# MASTERING MIXOLOGY

*Crafting The Perfect Classic Cocktails For Home Bartenders*
*The Art To Liquid Intelligence For Beginners*

## WHISKEY MORGAN

© **Copyright 2023 Whiskey Morgan- All rights reserved.**

The content contained within this book may not be reproduced, duplicated or transmitted without direct written permission from the author or the publisher.

Under no circumstances will any blame or legal responsibility be held against the publisher or author for any damages, reparation, or monetary loss due to the information contained within this book. Either directly or indirectly. You are responsible for your own choices, actions, and results.

**Legal Notice:**

This book is copyright protected. This book is only for personal use. You cannot amend, distribute, sell, use, quote or paraphrase any part or the content within this book without the consent of the author or publisher.

**Disclaimer Notice:**

Please note the information contained within this document is for educational and entertainment purposes only. All effort has been made to present accurate, up to date, and reliable, complete information. No warranties of any kind are declared or implied. Readers acknowledge that the author is not engaging in the rendering of legal, financial, medical, or professional advice. The content within this book has been derived from various sources. Please consult a licensed professional before attempting any techniques outlined in this book.

By reading this document, the reader agrees that under no circumstances is the author responsible for any losses, direct or indirect, which are incurred because of the use of the information contained within this document, including, but not limited to errors, omissions, or inaccuracies.

# TABLE OF CONTENTS

| | |
|---|---|
| *INTRODUCTION* | V |
| *ABOUT THE AUTHOR* | VI |
| *SPECIAL BONUS* | VIII |
| CHAPTER 1 | 1 |
|     HOW CLASSICS SHAPED HISTORY | 1 |
|     COCKTAIL EVOLUTION | 12 |
|     THE ROLE OF SPIRIT | 13 |
|     A TIMELESS APPEAL | 15 |
|     KEY TAKEAWAYS | 17 |
| CHAPTER 2 | 19 |
|     EQUIPMENT | 20 |
|     KEY TAKEAWAYS | 30 |
| CHAPTER 3 | 31 |
|     SPIRITS | 32 |
|     BITTERS | 35 |
|     LIQUEURS | 36 |
|     WINES | 37 |
|     GARNISHES | 38 |
|     MODIFIERS | 39 |
|     KEY TAKEAWAYS | 40 |
| CHAPTER 4 | 41 |
|     TECHNIQUE HISTORY | 45 |
|     A TALL DRINK OF HISTORY | 47 |
|     KEY TAKEAWAYS | 48 |
| CHAPTER 5 | 49 |

| | |
|---|---:|
| WHY RULES MATTER | 52 |
| A HISTORY OF RULES | 52 |
| KEY TAKEAWAYS | 53 |
| A SHORT MESSAGE FROM THE AUTHOR | 55 |
| **CHAPTER 6** | **57** |
| VODKA | 57 |
| GIN | 63 |
| WHITE RUM | 68 |
| WHITE WINE | 73 |
| WHEN TO USE THESE PREFERRED SPIRITS | 78 |
| SPIRIT HISTORY | 79 |
| KEY TAKEAWAYS | 79 |
| **CHAPTER 7** | **83** |
| WHISKEY | 83 |
| BOURBON | 89 |
| BRANDY | 94 |
| DARK RUM | 99 |
| RED WINE | 104 |
| WHEN TO USE THESE PREFERRED SPIRITS | 109 |
| SPIRIT HISTORY | 109 |
| KEY TAKEAWAYS | 110 |
| **CHAPTER 8** | **113** |
| KEY TAKEAWAYS | 124 |
| *CONCLUSION* | *127* |
| *A SHORT MESSAGE FROM THE AUTHOR* | *128* |

# INTRODUCTION

Are you tired of being intimidated by the art of mixology and feeling like you're missing out on the beauty of crafted cocktails? Do you find yourself avoiding them due to a lack of knowledge and understanding of the techniques and methods involved?

Uncover the secrets of mixology and elevate your home bar game to new heights with *"Mastering Mixology: Crafting the Perfect Classic Cocktails."* Impress your friends with expertly crafted cocktails that are balanced to perfection. From the crisp bite of a well-made martini to the smooth sweetness of a classic Old Fashioned, you'll learn the art of creating timeless drinks.

From the history and background to the process and techniques, by the end of this book, you will have the education and confidence to indulge in this fascinating world. Say goodbye to the scary learning curve, and embrace the art of crafting cocktails like a pro.

You'll learn everything you need to know about crafting the perfect cocktail. The book covers a wide range of topics, from studying the classics and understanding the history and styles of cocktails to curating your ingredients and learning the techniques and methods involved in mixology. You'll also discover the rules of mixology and gain access to a range of recipes for light and dark spirits as well as infused classic cocktails. Whether you're a beginner looking to enhance your skills or a seasoned bartender looking to expand your knowledge, this book will provide you with the tools and resources you need to become a master mixologist with your newfound expertise.

It's important to note that Mixology and Bartending will be used interchangeably in this book, where both will be spoken around the idea of crafting the perfect classic cocktail. This book will not fulfill the full extent of what mixology may entail such as molecular gastronomy and structural reforming through culinary technique.

Before we dive in, I want you to take a quick moment with me. I want you to picture a warm summer evening, when the sun is just beginning to set, and friends and family have gathered at your home for a celebration. With your newfound skills as a home bartender, you are able to craft exquisite cocktails that delight your guests, sparking conversation and laughter as you all share stories and create cherished memories together. As the night unfolds, you find a profound sense of joy and accomplishment in your ability to bring people together over expertly crafted drinks. By reading this book, this is what I want you to accomplish. Speaking from the experience of a seasoned bartender, this feeling is truly unmatched. So without further ado, let's dive in!

## ABOUT THE AUTHOR

Whiskey Morgan is a seasoned mixologist and bartender with over 15 years of experience in the industry. Growing up in a family of mixologist connoisseurs, he fell in love with the craft of creating timeless cocktails at a young age. After working his way up through the ranks of various high-end bars and restaurants, he turned his attention to sharing his knowledge and passion for cocktail mixology through the written word. His dedication to the craft and unwavering commitment to quality have earned him a reputation as one of the most knowledgeable and respected mixologists in the industry.

This book is a comprehensive guide for those looking to learn about classic cocktails and the art of mixology. It is designed to educate beginners on the history of cocktails, as well as the techniques and methods required to become a skilled at-home bartender. However, it is important to note that this book is specifically focused on mixology and does not cover any other topics outside of this realm.

Now that you have a better understanding of what this book is all about, it's time to dive into the world of mixology. Let's start by exploring the classics and uncovering the history and styles of cocktails that have stood the test of time. Turn the page and let's get started on your journey to becoming a master mixologist!

# SPECIAL BONUS

Want this Bonus book for Free?

Get FREE, unlimited access to it and all of my new books by joining the Fan Base!

Click or Scan the barcode to Join!

# CHAPTER 1

## Studying The Classics

Step back in time and explore the rich history of cocktails. In this chapter, we'll take a deep dive into the classics and discover the timeless styles and recipes that have stood the test of time. From the origins of mixology to the evolution of cocktails, you'll gain a newfound appreciation for the art of crafting the perfect drink.

In this chapter, we'll delve into the world of classic cocktails and explore the history and evolution of mixology. From the origins of cocktail culture to the timeless styles that have stood the test of time, you'll gain a deeper understanding of the classic drinks that have defined the industry. By the end of this chapter, you'll have a solid foundation of knowledge on the classics and be ready to start experimenting with your own creations.

**HOW CLASSICS SHAPED HISTORY**

Let's take a closer look at the history and evolution of the top to classic cocktails and how these shaped the art of mixology and bartending. To define "classic," we're referring to drinks that have been around for many years and have stood the test of time. They have a timeless appeal and are considered the building blocks of mixology. The top 10 classic cocktails we'll be covering in detail are:

- Martini
- Old Fashioned
- Manhattan
- Daiquiri
- Margarita
- Sazerac
- Negroni
- Gin Fizz
- Whiskey Sour
- Sidecar

In this section we'll explore a composition of items including each cocktail's origins, its ingredients, the evolution of each and how the cocktails are presently used today. With a solid understanding of the classics, you'll be ready to start experimenting with your own creations.

***Martini:*** The Martini is an iconic cocktail with roots dating back to the late 19th century. Typically made with equal parts gin and vermouth in chilled glasses and garnished with an olive, its original recipe called for a 2:1 ratio between those ingredients which created a delicate balance between botanical notes of gin and herbal flavors of vermouth.

As time went on, the Martini evolved to meet differing tastes and preferences. One key change was the addition of vodka as a base spirit - leading to its creation as the Vodka Martini. This variant swapped out gin for vodka for a smoother and more neutral flavor profile - eventually becoming popular during mid-20th century as an icon of sophistication and glamour. Another popular variation is the Dirty Martini, which adds olive brine for an unexpected briny and salty note in their martinis. Garnished with one or more olives for visual flair.

Bartenders and mixologists alike have become adept at taking the Martini to new heights over recent years, experimenting with various ingredients and techniques. Some variations feature citrus- or botanical-infused vodka or gin spirits as a creative twist, as well as garnishes such as lemon twists or even pickled vegetables for extra aroma and visual flair.

Though its creation and variations may have changed over the years, the Martini remains a timeless classic in cocktail culture, celebrated for its timeless beauty and versatility. Be it at a fancy lounge or simply mixed at home - its refined simplicity continues to charm cocktail enthusiasts as its endless possibilities allow them to customize it according to individual tastes and needs.

 ***Old Fashioned:*** Dating back to the late 1800s, the Old Fashioned cocktail has an esteemed legacy dating back decades. Its name encapsulates its classic approach to mixology - created to highlight whiskey's true flavors without adding unnecessary garnishments.

Original Old Fashioneds combined sugar, bitters, water and whiskey into one glass before skillful mixing to achieve an aromatic yet sweet elixir. Individuals would sometimes garnish their drinks with lemon peels or cherries to add visual allure and citrus notes; personal preferences were usually dictated in selecting their whiskey of choice with rye being often preferred over others.

Over its history, the Old Fashioned has undergone many variations and modifications. Brandy, gin, and even rum have all been used to enhance its flavor profile; nevertheless, its original version remains highly valued.

Crafting the ideal Old Fashioned requires striking a delicate balance between sweetness, bitterness and whiskey's unique profile. Selecting premium spirits, aromatic bitters and natural sweeteners of high quality is key for crafting this drink. Stirring with ice can be beneficial in reaching desired dilution and temperature levels before straining into chilled glasses to provide a delightful drinking experience.

Recently, the Old Fashioned has experienced a revival in popularity among both bartenders and cocktail enthusiasts alike. Craft cocktail bars and speakeasies often present their own interpretation of this exquisite drink with distinctive bitters, syrups, or garnishes to give their own flair; nonetheless its essence remains unaltered: an elegant drink which honors whiskey in its unadulterated state without overindulgence or extraneous bitters.

 ***Manhattan:*** Like many classic cocktails, its exact origins remain debatable, though most agree it first gained widespread acclaim in New York's Borough of Manhattan during the late 19th century.

To create the original Manhattan cocktail, one would combine whiskey, sweet vermouth and aromatic bitters in a mixing glass and strain into chilled coupe or martini glasses before garnishing them with maraschino cherries for visual and sensory appeal.

Traditional Manhattans were made using rye whiskey; however, more recently bourbon has gained in popularity as an alternative. Both types of whiskey impart unique flavor profiles; for instance rye is known for its dry finish while bourbon boasts sweeter and riper characteristics.

Like other classic cocktails, the Manhattan has undergone various adaptations and interpretations throughout its history. One notable variation is the Perfect Manhattan which combines equal amounts of sweet and dry vermouth for an ideal balance. By contrast, its Dry Manhattan variant substitutes sweet vermouth for dry vermouth to produce a lighter and more herbaceous version.

Modern bartenders and mixologists have increasingly shown their creativity when crafting Manhattans. They have experimented with different bitters, aged spirits, garnishes with subtle differences and more complex cocktails such as including blanc vermouth or herbal liqueurs to give extra depth and complexity to the drink.

The Manhattan is a timeless classic cocktail, beloved for its sophisticated yet lasting appeal. Combining whiskey and vermouth continues to enthrall cocktail enthusiasts worldwide; whether sipped at intimate lounges or expertly mixed at home. Its legacy and artistry remain undiminished.

***Daiquiri:*** Daiquiris can be traced back to a 19th-century mining town on Cuba's southeast coast, but has since gained global acclaim as a beloved choice among cocktail enthusiasts. They were originally enjoyed as an indulgence made up of just three ingredients - rum, lime juice and sugar - but their popularity quickly spread among both Cubans and American expatriates who visited Cuba. Cuban varieties like Havana Club brought added subtle yet unique flavors into the recipe.

Ernest Hemingway played a vital role in spreading the fame of Daiquiris beyond Cuba. While in Havana, Hemingway became an avid admirer and helped the drink become well known internationally. Variations such as Hemingway Daiquiri or Papa Doble cocktails soon emerged in his honor, mixing grapefruit juice with maraschino liqueur.

Daiquris soon proved their adaptability as bartenders experimented with different flavors and fruits. A signature creation is the Strawberry Daiquiri which features fresh strawberries combined with sugar for a visually stunning and sweet experience perfect for cocktail connoisseurs looking for an exquisite drink experience.

Frozen Daiquiris were an exciting development of the traditional Daiquiri cocktail. By adding crushed ice, bartenders could increase its refreshing and invigorating properties and make this treat particularly popular in warm-weather locations where it provided welcome relief from heat stress.

Daiquiris continue to progress worldwide as bartenders experiment with various fruits, herbs, and spices to craft unique Daiquiri variations. Such innovations have yielded tantalizing combinations like mango, pineapple, coconut, and passion fruit for an infinite number of flavor profiles - an evolution which may take another 100 years!

The Daiquiri has earned itself a worldwide following as an irresistibly refreshing classic cocktail, popular across cultures and generations alike. Enjoyed both in its original form or via various innovative interpretations that have arisen, its long history and versatility have cemented its legacy among cocktail enthusiasts; be it on a sandy beach or trendy cocktail bar; its delightful combination of sweetness, tartness and rum-infused goodness never ceases to delight and refresh!

***Margarita:*** While its exact roots may be controversial, most experts agree it gained prominence during the 1940s and 50s in the United States. Originally composed of tequila, lime juice, and triple sec liqueur (an orange-flavored orangey beverage), these ingredients would then be mixed together with ice and shaken together until chilled before straining into glasses with salt-rimmed rims for enhanced flavors and sensory experiences. A lime wedge was often added for visual interest as well as acidity or acidity!

The Margarita has evolved to encompass various ingredients and flavors. Bartenders and mixologists have experimented with adding fruit such as strawberries, mangoes, and pineapple for fruit-infused Margaritas; watermelons or passion fruit syrup has also been added for sweetness and complexity; spicy variations using ingredients like jalapenos or chili peppers has become popular as they add an additional spiced kick.

Finding the ideal Margarita recipe requires finding the ideal balance of tequila, lime juice and triple sec. Selecting high-quality ingredients such as premium tequilas and freshly squeezed lime juice can significantly enhance flavor, creating an exceptional Margarita experience. Some prefer tarter versions featuring higher concentrations of lime juice while others may enjoy sweeter versions featuring an addition of agave syrup or simple syrup for sweetness.

The Margarita has quickly become one of the world's favorite cocktails, becoming an internationally beloved icon. Its name alone conjures images of beach vacations, Mexican cuisine and festive celebrations; serving it on rocks or frozen blend is possible or aged for added complexity in barrels for maximum pleasure - whether sipped at lively beach bars or simply enjoyed in one's own backyard, its refreshing and vibrant nature continues to draw drink enthusiasts all around.

***Sazerac:*** The Sazerac has a long history dating back to New Orleans during the mid 19th century. Its creation can be traced to Antoine Peychaud, a pharmacist who used his homemade bitters in creating concoctions known as Sazeracs for friends to drink - becoming known later as one of New Orleans' signature drinks.

Original versions of the Sazerac were typically composed with cognac as its base spirit; French brandy cognac was often chosen for cocktails at this time. But as American culture increasingly adopted rye whiskey for drinking purposes, so too did its presence in Sazerac recipes; as this occurred, its introduction greatly contributed to creating its modern form.

The classic Sazerac cocktail features rye whiskey, sugar, Peychaud's bitters (named for their creator Antoine Peychaud), and absinthe. Sugar should first be mushed together with several dashes of Peychaud's bitters before mixing in the rye whiskey. Rinsing out your glass with absinthe then gives this cocktail its subtle herbaceous and anise notes before stirring with ice to strain into an old-fashioned glass with lemon twist added at last step to release its fragrant aromatic notes!

One of the distinguishing elements of the Sazerac cocktail is its use of absinthe, an aromatic and herbaceous spirit which was once controversial and even banned in many countries due to its perceived hallucinogenic properties. Modern absinthe used for cocktails contains significantly reduced levels of psychoactive compound thujone and can safely be consumed when added into cocktails like the Sazerac. Absinthe adds not only distinctive flavor, but also provides an immersive visual experience when swirling the drink and experiencing its "louche effect", when its components cloud over and release their aromas!

The Sazerac's place in cocktail history cannot be overstated. It stands as an exemplary demonstration of balance and layering flavors. Combining spicy rye whiskey with sweet sugar syrup, complex Peychaud's bitters and aromatic absinthe creates an exciting drink with plenty of character that leaves its mark.

The journey of this drink has created variations such as using different kinds of whiskey or brandy as the base spirit have arisen; yet its timeless recipe remains unchanged, serving as a testament to this historic cocktail's enduring legacy and being enjoyed widely among cocktail enthusiasts and visitors to New Orleans where it stands as a beloved symbol of their city's rich cocktail history.

 *Negroni:* The Negroni is a timeless cocktail with a long and distinguished history dating back to Italy during the early 20th century. Its creation can often be traced to Count Camillo Negroni, an Italian nobleman with an affinity for cocktails who visited Florence where bartender Fosco Scarselli replaced soda water with gin in order to create something stronger than its predecessor Americano and thus gave birth to its signature drink: the Negroni.

The classic Negroni recipe calls for equal parts gin, sweet vermouth and Campari-- an iconic Italian bitter liqueur--in order to achieve the optimal harmony of flavors between their three components: herbal citrus notes in the gin; rich and nuanced sweetness from vermouth and Campari's unmistakable bitter profile; all while being stirred over ice until desired dilution and temperature is reached, before straining into rocks glass over fresh ice for serving with an orange twist for added vibrance!

Negroni cocktails stand apart from classic cocktails in that they contain Campari. A vibrant red liqueur with an distinctive bitter flavor made from herbs, spices and fruits derived in Italy's Veneto region, Campari provides a delightful and refreshing balance that appeals to adventurous palates.

As time has progressed, the Negroni has gained tremendous renown and become a canvas for experimentation and reinvention. Bartenders and cocktail enthusiasts have introduced variations that showcase its adaptability; for instance, using different types of gin such as barrel-aged or botanical-infused varieties can add depth and complexity; some enthusiasts even replace it with other spirits like bourbon or tequila for even greater creativity while still maintaining its signature bitter taste.

***Gin Fizz:*** Dating back to the 19th century, ts origin can be credited to bartenders' creative ingenuity when it came to crafting refreshing and effervescent drinks for their patrons. The original Gin Fizz recipes consist of gin, lemon juice, sugar, and soda water for maximum citrus, sweetness, and fizziness.

Gin Fizz cocktails were unique among their time due to their preparation. Bartenders would frequently shake vigorously using "dry shaking," an uncommon practice whereby ingredients are shaken without ice to produce frothy textures that created creamy foam on top of each cocktail - something which set it apart from other similar drinks of its day. This technique gave rise to one of its hallmark features of this drink - its signature foam head.

Gin Fizz's popularity can be attributed to its light and refreshing flavor profile. Gin's botanical notes from its production using juniper berries and other botanicals provides a signature aroma while fresh lemon juice provides bright citrus notes while sugar balances acidity with sweetness, adding another dimension of balance and refreshment to this cocktail. Finally, soda water gives this drink its fizziness for added pleasure!

The Gin Fizz has evolved to incorporate variations with other citrus juices such as lime or grapefruit juice to provide more complex and varied flavors. Some also utilize sweet syrups like raspberry or elderflower that add a subtle hint of sweetness or complexity - yet its classic combination of gin, lemon juice, sugar, and soda water remains popular with cocktail enthusiasts.

Gin Fizz's versatility and adaptability have cemented its place as a timeless classic that transcends seasons and occasions. Particularly popular during warmer months, its light citrus flavor serves as the ideal thirst-quencher. No matter whether enjoyed at a bustling cocktail bar, rooftop terrace party, backyard get together or backyard party; drinkers continue to adore its refreshing taste and delicious foamy texture!

***Whiskey Sour:*** Whiskey Sours have an intriguing past dating back to late 19th-century America, during a time when cocktails became increasingly popular and mixology emerged as an art form.

Original Whiskey Sour was an easy yet effective cocktail to create, combining whiskey, lemon juice, sugar, and egg white into one delicious drink. Whiskey provided the main spirit that set the stage for this drink while freshly squeezed lemon juice added an acidic citrus element that balanced out its complexity perfectly with sugar as sweetener; adding egg white brought velvety textures that enhanced overall drinking experiences and provided velvety smoothness that enhanced drinking experiences further still.

Whiskey Sours first achieved great popularity during Prohibition (1920-1933). Due to poor-quality bootleg whiskey available during that era, many sought a way to mask any unpleasant flavors present in illegal spirits such as bootleg whiskey. A perfect balance between ingredients allowed them to successfully mask harsh or rough characteristics and enable consumers to enjoy whiskey without its unpleasant aftertaste.

Assembling the ideal Whiskey Sour requires finding an ideal balance of ingredients. Whiskey quality has an enormous effect on its flavor profile; popular choices for this cocktail include bourbon and rye whiskeys. Utilizing freshly squeezed lemon juice with high-grade sugar ensures bright citrus sweetness; while shaking an egg white vigorously adds an luxurious element. While garnishes for a Whiskey Sour usually include cherries and orange slices as these additions add both visual appeal and fruity flavors that complement the overall profile of this refreshing drink.

This classic have arisen to meet different tastes and preferences. Some include adding other citrus juices such as lime or grapefruit juice for additional flavors while other incorporate honey or maple flavored syrups for depth and complexity. Still, its timeless combination of whiskey, lemon juice, sugar, and egg white remains popular with cocktail enthusiasts.

The Whiskey Sour remains a classic cocktail enjoyed both in bars and at home. With its timeless appeal, balanced flavor profile, and refreshing beverage qualities, its appeal to cocktail enthusiasts continues to remain strong making it an irresistibly refreshing drink!

 ***Sidecar:*** The Sidecar cocktail, first invented in early 20th-century France, has an intricate history. Although its precise origins remain unclear, many believe that its popularity spread quickly among cocktail enthusiasts and socialites, ultimately becoming one of their go-to drinks.

To craft the original Sidecar cocktail, three key ingredients were necessary: cognac, triple sec and lemon juice. Cognac's luxurious French brandy background gave this drink its luxurious character while infusing sweetness and depth into it. Triple sec added some additional sweetness while fresh-squeezed lemon juice added refreshing citrusy zing that balanced out its rich spirits nicely.

Traditional Sidecar cocktails were served in glasses rimmed with sugar for enhanced visual appeal and an elevated drinking experience. A final flourish would include adding a twist of lemon to release its aromatic citrus oils into the cocktail and provide an alluring finish touch.

Variations have emerged over time, using additional citrus juices such as lime or grapefruit juices to provide distinct flavor profiles and various spirits such as brandy or whiskey as base spirits. Yet the original formula featuring cognac, triple sec, and lemon juice remains elegantly well-balanced - an option beloved by many cocktail enthusiasts alike.

The Sidecar is beloved among those who appreciate complex yet harmonious flavors, boasting velvety cognac, creamy triple sec, and tart lemon juice to form an intoxicating beverage that exudes sophistication without compromising accessibility. A favorite among sophisticated drinkers, its combination of carefully chosen ingredients exemplifies mixology's artistry in creating this perfect drinking experience.

The Sidecar has long been an elegant staple in bars and cocktail lounges worldwide due to its timeless charm and exquisitely balanced flavors. Be it an aperitif or evening drink, the Sidecar remains an exceptional drinking experience that invites connoisseurs of sophisticated pleasures to experience its exquisite drinking pleasures.

The top 10 classic cocktails we've outlined have had a profound impact on the mixology industry and helped shape the art of cocktail making. These drinks have stood the test of time and continue to be popular choices at bars and restaurants around the world. They have set the standard for what a well-made cocktail should be and have influenced the development of new and innovative drinks.

For example, the Martini has become synonymous with sophistication and elegance, and its simple yet classic recipe has been a favorite of bartenders for generations. The Old Fashioned, on the other hand, is a drink that has undergone many transformations over the years, but its timeless appeal remains unchanged. The Manhattan, with its smooth and well-balanced flavor, has been a staple of cocktail culture for over a century.

Each of these classic cocktails has a unique history and story, and they have all played a significant role in shaping the mixology industry. By studying the classics, you'll gain a deeper appreciation for the art of cocktail making and understand how these timeless drinks have influenced the development of new and innovative drinks.

## COCKTAIL EVOLUTION

Cocktails have undergone a significant evolution over the years, adapting to changing tastes and trends in the mixology industry. From the early days of cocktail culture, when drinks were simple combinations of spirits and mixers, to the modern era of mixology, where bartenders are experimenting with new ingredients and techniques, cocktails have come a long way.

In the early 20th century, cocktails became more sophisticated, with the addition of ingredients like bitters, liqueurs, and syrups. This opened a whole new world of flavor combinations, and bartenders began to experiment with new and innovative drinks. As the industry continued to evolve, bartenders began to focus on presentation, using creative garnishes and serving drinks in unique and visually stunning glassware.

Today, the mixology industry is more innovative and diverse than ever before, with bartenders pushing the boundaries of what a cocktail can be. From molecular mixology to the use of unconventional ingredients like herbs, spices, and fruits, the possibilities are endless. With this evolution, the classics continue to adapt and change, but they remain at the heart of cocktail culture, serving as a foundation for new and innovative drinks.

## THE ROLE OF SPIRIT

These ingredients have played a critical role in the evolution of cocktail culture and have helped to shape the industry as we know it today.

Vermouth is a type of fortified wine that is flavored with various herbs, spices, and fruits. It originated in Italy in the late 1700s and was used as a medicinal drink. Over time, vermouth became popular as an ingredient in cocktails, including the Martini and Manhattan. Vermouth is available in two types: sweet (red) vermouth and dry (white) vermouth.

Bitters are made by infusing various botanicals and spices in alcohol. Bitters have been used for centuries as a digestive aid and were first used in cocktails in the early 19th century. Today, bitters are used to add depth, complexity, and balance to drinks.

Tequila is made from the blue agave plant, which is native to Mexico. Tequila has been produced in Mexico for over 400 years and has become a popular spirit worldwide. Tequila is used in a variety of cocktails, including the Margarita and Paloma, and is often enjoyed on its own as a shot or sipped neat.

Cognac is a type of brandy that is produced in the Cognac region of France. Cognac is made from distilled white wine and is aged in oak barrels, which gives it its distinctive flavor. Cognac has been produced for over 400 years and is used in a variety of cocktails, including the Sidecar and French 75.

Absinthe is made from a mixture of herbs, including wormwood, anise, and fennel. Absinthe originated in Switzerland in the late 18th century and became popular in France in the 19th century. Absinthe was banned in many countries in the early 20th century due to its high alcohol content and reputation for causing hallucinations, but it has since been re-legalized in many countries and has regained popularity as an ingredient in cocktails.

Campari is a type of bitter liqueur that is produced in Italy. Campari is made from a blend of herbs, spices, and fruits and is known for its bitter, slightly sweet flavor. Campari is often enjoyed on its own as an aperitif.

Cointreau is a type of triple sec liqueur that is produced in France. Cointreau is made from a blend of sweet and bitter orange peels and is known for its sweet, citrus flavor. Cointreau is used in a variety of cocktails, including the Margarita and Sidecar, and is often enjoyed on its own as a digestif.

Vodka is a clear, neutral spirit that is made from a variety of grains, including wheat, rye, and corn. Vodka originated in Eastern Europe in the 9th century and has since become a popular spirit worldwide. Vodka is used in a variety of cocktails, including the Martini and Cosmopolitan, and is often enjoyed on its own as a shot or mixed with juice or soda.

Gin is made by distilling neutral spirits with juniper berries and other botanicals. Gin originated in the Netherlands in the 17th century and has since become a popular spirit worldwide. Gin is used in a variety of cocktails, including the Martini and Gin Fizz, and is often enjoyed on its own as a gin and tonic.

Bourbon is a type of whiskey that is made from a mixture of grains, including corn, rye, and barley. Bourbon must be aged in new, charred oak barrels for at least two years to be considered bourbon. Bourbon originated in the United States in the late 1700s and is primarily produced in Kentucky.

Scotch is a type of whiskey that is made from malted barley and must be aged in oak casks for at least three years. Scotch is produced in Scotland and is divided into two types: single malt scotch, which is made from 100% malted barley, and blended scotch, which is made from a mixture of single malt scotch and grain whiskey.

Brandy is made by distilling wine. Brandy is available in a variety of styles, including Cognac, which is produced in France, and American brandy, which is produced in the United States. Brandy is used in a variety of cocktails, including the Sidecar and French 75, and is often enjoyed on its own as a digestif.

Rum is made from sugar cane or molasses. Rum is available in a variety of styles, including white rum, which is light and crisp, and dark rum, which is aged and has a stronger flavor. Rum is used in a variety of cocktails, including the Daiquiri and Mai Tai, and is often enjoyed on its own as a rum and cola.

Each of these spirits and liquors has its own unique flavor profile, and they play a critical role in the flavor and balance of classic cocktails. By understanding the history and background of these ingredients, you'll gain a deeper appreciation for the art of cocktail making and be able to create drinks that are well-balanced and true to the classics.

**A TIMELESS APPEAL**

Cocktails have a timeless appeal that has captured the imagination of people for generations. From their rich history and evolution to the art and science of mixology, there is so much to love about these classic drinks.

One of the things that makes cocktails so special is their ability to evoke emotions and memories. Whether it's sipping a Martini at a fancy bar, sharing a Whiskey Sour with friends, or indulging in a classic Old Fashioned after a long day, cocktails have the power to create experiences and memories that last a lifetime.

Another aspect of cocktails that makes them so special is their versatility. With a wide range of ingredients and techniques, bartenders can create an endless array of flavors and combinations, each with its own unique character and appeal. Whether you prefer sweet, sour, bitter, or smoky flavors, there is a cocktail out there that is sure to suit your tastes.

Finally, the art of cocktail making is both a science and an art. From the precise measurements and techniques used to create the perfect balance of flavors to the creative presentation and garnishes that make each drink a work of art, mixology is a fascinating and endlessly entertaining subject. Whether you're a beginner or a seasoned bartender, there is always something new to learn and discover in the world of cocktails.

Whether you're looking to impress your friends with your newfound skills or simply looking to indulge in the timeless appeal of classic cocktails, this is the guide you need to get started.

One of the most interesting facts about the history of cocktails is the role that bartenders have played in their evolution. In the early days of cocktail culture, bartenders were more than just mixologists; they were also chemists, inventors, and entrepreneurs. They were constantly experimenting with new ingredients and techniques, and they were always on the lookout for ways to create new and innovative drinks.

One famous example is Jerry Thomas, considered by many to be the father of American mixology. He was a bartender in the mid-19th century and was known for his creative and inventive cocktails. He was the first bartender to use a cocktail shaker and created many of the classic cocktails we know and love today, including the Martini and the Manhattan.

Thomas's legacy lives on, and he continues to inspire bartenders around the world who are dedicated to preserving the art of cocktail making and pushing the boundaries of what is possible. This is just one of the many fascinating stories that demonstrate the rich history and evolution of cocktails and the important role that bartenders have played in their development.

## KEY TAKEAWAYS

The classics have played a critical role in shaping the mixology industry and continue to be a favorite among bartenders and cocktail enthusiasts. From the history and evolution of these timeless drinks to the ingredients and techniques used to make them, this chapter has provided a comprehensive overview of what makes a classic cocktail. By understanding the key takeaways and the important role that spirits and liquors play in the flavor and balance of these drinks, you'll be well on your way to becoming a true mixology master.

The key takeaways from this chapter included:

- The definition of "classic cocktails" and their significance in the mixology industry.
- The history and evolution of the top 10 classic cocktails.
- The role of spirits and liquors in the flavor and balance of classic cocktails.
- The importance of understanding the history and background of cocktails in order to create well-balanced and true-to-the-classics drinks.
- The timeless appeal of cocktails and the role that bartenders have played in their development.

You're ready to start experimenting with your own creations. Raise your glass and celebrate the timeless appeal of the classics. Cheers to many delicious cocktails to come!

With your newfound knowledge of the classics, it's time to take your cocktail game to the next level. In the next chapter, we'll be diving into the tools and equipment you'll need to create your own at-home bartending station. From glassware to shakers to strainers, you'll learn everything you need to know to set up your own bar and start making your favorite drinks. So, let's get started and find out what it takes to become a true at-home bartender!

# CHAPTER 2

## The 'At Home' Bartender

In this chapter, we'll equip you with everything you need to set up your very own cocktail station. From the basics of bar supplies to the different types of glassware, you'll learn how to stock your bar like a pro and serve up classic cocktails with ease. Get ready to impress your friends and family with your newfound mixology skills!

The focus will be on the essential equipment and tools needed to create a fully stocked home bar and will cover the following topics in detail:

Essential bar equipment: This section will provide a comprehensive list of all the equipment required to set up a functional home bar, including shakers, strainers, jiggers, bar spoons, cutting boards, bottle openers, and more.

Types of glassware: In this section, the different types of glassware used in mixology will be described, including martini glasses, whiskey tumblers, highball glasses, and others. The uses of each type of glassware will be explained and you'll be provided with tips on how to choose the right glassware for your needs.

Choosing the right equipment: This section will provide tips on how to choose the right equipment for your home bar. You'll be advised on what to consider when making equipment purchases, such as budget, frequency of use, and personal style.

# Mastering Mixology

By the end of this chapter, you'll have explored the essential equipment needed to set up a fully functioning home bar. From shakers to strainers, we'll go through the must-have tools that every aspiring home bartender should have in their arsenal. Whether you're just starting out or looking to upgrade your current setup, this chapter will provide you with a comprehensive guide to setting up the perfect at-home bar. We'll also touch on the different types of glassware that are essential for serving up classic cocktails, and how to choose the right glasses for each drink. Get ready to take your home bartending skills to the next level with this comprehensive guide to the at-home bar.

## EQUIPMENT

***Shakers:*** Cocktail shakers are essential for creating a well-mixed drink. You can choose from classic metal shakers or the more modern, versatile Boston shakers.

***Strainers:*** Strainers are used to remove ice and other ingredients from your drink after shaking or stirring. A Hawthorne strainer is a classic option, while a julep strainer is great for muddled drinks.

***Jiggers:*** Jiggers are used to measure out precise amounts of ingredients for your cocktails. A double jigger is ideal, allowing you to measure both 1.5 oz and 1 oz portions.

***Bar Spoons:*** Bar spoons are long-handled spoons that make stirring cocktails easier. Look for a twisted handle option for added grip.

***Cutting Boards:*** A cutting board is a must-have for any home bar. Use it to chop fruits, herbs, and other garnishes for your cocktails.

***Bottle Openers:*** You'll need a bottle opener for any bottled drinks you serve, including beer, soda, and wine.

***Glassware:*** Glassware is important for both presentation and function. Basic glassware for a home bar should include martini glasses, highball glasses, rocks glasses, and shot glasses.

***Ice Buckets:*** An ice bucket is essential for keeping your ice from melting quickly. Look for an insulated option to keep your ice colder for longer.

***Muddler:*** A muddler is used to crush and mix ingredients in the bottom of your glass.

***Bar Towels:*** Bar towels are important for cleaning up spills and wiping down surfaces.

***Ice Cube Trays:*** Ice cube trays are a must-have for making sure you always have enough ice on hand.

***Blender:*** A blender is a useful tool for creating frozen cocktails.

Having all of these pieces of equipment on hand will ensure that you have everything you need to create classic cocktails at home.

## Shakers

In the world of mixology, shakers play a crucial role in creating perfectly blended cocktails. There are several different types of shakers, each with its own unique features and benefits. Here are some of the most common types:

***Boston Shaker:*** This is a two-piece shaker that consists of a large metal tin and a smaller mixing glass. The glass fits snugly into the tin, creating a tight seal for shaking cocktails.

***Cobbler Shaker:*** This is a three-piece shaker that consists of a metal tin, a strainer, and a cap. The cap has a built-in strainer, making it easy to strain cocktails without having to use a separate strainer.

 ***French Shaker:*** This is a two-piece shaker that consists of a metal tin and a strainer. The strainer fits onto the top of the tin, creating a tight seal for shaking cocktails.

Each type of shaker has its own unique features and benefits, so it's important to choose the right one for your specific needs and preferences.

## Strainers

There are several types of strainers, each with a different function.

 The Hawthorne strainer is a metal strainer with a spring that fits into a shaker tin and is commonly used to strain shaken cocktails.

 The Julep strainer is a perforated metal cup that fits over the rim of a mixing glass and is used to strain stirred cocktails.

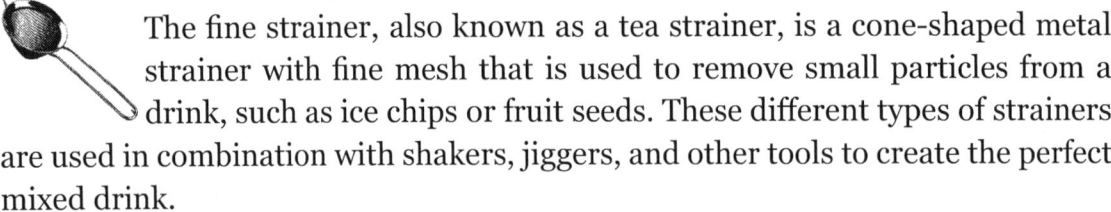 The fine strainer, also known as a tea strainer, is a cone-shaped metal strainer with fine mesh that is used to remove small particles from a drink, such as ice chips or fruit seeds. These different types of strainers are used in combination with shakers, jiggers, and other tools to create the perfect mixed drink.

## Jiggers

Small, hourglass-shaped measuring devices used to accurately measure the volume of spirits and other ingredients in a cocktail, jiggers come in a variety of sizes, but the most common sizes are 1/2 oz and 1 oz. They are usually made of stainless steel and are designed double-ended, allowing bartenders to measure two different amounts of liquid at once. Jiggers are essential for achieving consistent, balanced cocktails and are a must-have tool for any aspiring home bartender.

## Bar Spoons

Long, thin spoons with a twisted handle that are used for stirring drinks and layering ingredients. Bar spoons are typically made of stainless steel and are designed with a long handle to reach the bottom of tall cocktail glasses. The twisted handle allows for a comfortable grip, making it easier to stir drinks for an extended period of time. Additionally, some bar spoons feature a flat disc on the end, which is useful for muddling ingredients or layering drinks. Bar spoons are an indispensable tool for any home bartender, as they help ensure that drinks are properly mixed and layered for the best possible flavor and presentation.

## Cutting Boards

These are used to prepare fruits, herbs, and other ingredients for cocktails. There are several types of cutting boards available, including plastic, bamboo, and wooden boards. The choice of cutting board will depend on personal preference and the type of ingredients being prepared. Bamboo cutting boards are a popular option due to their durability and eco-friendliness. Wooden boards, on the other hand, are more traditional and can offer a classic look to any bar setup. Plastic cutting boards are the most affordable option, but they are not as durable as bamboo or wooden boards. Regardless of the type of cutting board used, it is important to keep it clean and sanitized to prevent contamination of ingredients.

## Bottle Openers

A bottle opener is a tool that is used to open a bottle, typically a glass bottle that has a metal cap. This tool is a staple in any bar and is essential for opening any type of bottle, including beer and soda bottles, as well as liquor bottles with metal caps. Bottle openers come in many shapes and sizes, from simple flat-bottomed devices to elaborate multi-tool designs. Some bottle openers are designed specifically for opening beer bottles, while others are designed to open both beer and soda bottles. A good bottle opener should be durable, easy to use, and have a comfortable grip for quick and effortless opening.

## Glassware

In this section, we will discuss the different types of glassware used in mixology and their specific purposes. From martini glasses to highball glasses, each type of glass has its own unique shape and design to enhance the flavor and presentation of different cocktails. Whether you're serving up a classic martini or a refreshing gin and tonic, having the right glassware can make all the difference in the overall experience of your cocktail.

When it comes to mixology, the type of glassware used is just as important as the ingredients in the drink. Each type of glassware serves a specific purpose and enhances the drinking experience. Some of the most common types of glassware used in mixology include:

***Martini Glass:*** This iconic V-shaped glass is used to serve martinis and other chilled cocktails. Legend has it that the original Martini was served in a straight-sided glass, but bartender Martini di Arma di Taggia of the Knickerbocker Hotel in New York City added the V-shape to the glass to give it a more elegant and sophisticated look. This simple change in glassware transformed the Martini from just another drink to a classic cocktail, and the V-shaped Martini glass has since become a staple in mixology. This story highlights the importance of presentation and attention to detail in creating the perfect cocktail, which starts with the right glassware.

***Highball Glass:*** This tall, cylindrical glass is used to serve drinks that are made with a higher ratio of mixer to alcohol, such as a gin and tonic. The highball glass has become a staple in the world of mixology. It is typically used for serving long drinks, such as highballs and cocktails that are made with a large amount of ice, soda water, or other mixers. The glass is designed to allow these ingredients to be poured in without spilling, while also providing enough room for ice to be added without overflowing.

The highball glass gets its name from the popular highball cocktail, which is made by mixing a spirit with ice and soda water. The term highball is believed to have originated in the late 19th century, and the glassware style quickly became popular in the early 20th century. Highball glasses were typically made from glass or crystal and were designed with straight sides and a small base to allow for stacking.

One unique detail about the use of highball glasses is that they are often used to serve drinks that are meant to be enjoyed quickly, such as a gin and tonic or a rum and cola. The tall, cylindrical shape of the glass helps to keep the ingredients well-mixed, and the wide top allows for easy sipping. Additionally, the highball glass is often used to serve cocktails that are light and refreshing, making it a versatile option for any home bar.

**Rocks Glass:** Also known as an Old Fashioned glass, this short, wide glass is used to serve drinks that are meant to be sipped over ice, such as a whiskey sour. The tumbler is typically used for serving cocktails on the rocks, meaning with ice. Its wide, rounded shape allows for plenty of room for ice and is perfect for drinks such as the Old-Fashioned or Whiskey Sour. The history of the rocks glass can be traced back to the late 19th century when bartenders began serving drinks on the rocks as a way to cool down their beverages and add a touch of dilution to enhance the flavors. The rocks glass has remained a staple in the cocktail world, and its versatility and durability make it a must-have for any home bar.

**Champagne Flute:** This tall, narrow glass is specifically designed for serving sparkling wine or Champagne. It has a long stem to keep the drink away from the body heat and a narrow rim to retain the bubbles and aroma of the wine. The shape of the flute is important to enhance the drinking experience by highlighting the delicate flavors and aromas of the wine. The first Champagne flute was created in the 1690s and was designed to showcase the wine's bubbles and elegance. Today, the flute is a staple in any bar and is often used for special occasions and celebrations. A unique detail about its use is that the flute is often used to make the iconic cocktail, the Champagne Cocktail, which involves mixing sugar, bitters, and Champagne in the flute glass.

***Collins Glass:*** Similar to a highball glass, this tall, cylindrical glass is used to serve drinks that are made with a higher ratio of mixer to alcohol, such as a Tom Collins, and is typically used for cocktails that are served over ice and topped with soda water. This glass is named after the classic Collins cocktail, which is made with gin, lemon juice, sugar, and soda water. The shape of the Collins glass allows for the ingredients to be easily stirred and the carbonated soda water to be added to the top, creating a light and refreshing drink. The first appearance of the Collins glass in the cocktail world is unclear, but it has been a staple in mixology since the mid-19th century and remains a popular choice for many classic and contemporary cocktails.

***Coupe Glass:*** This shallow, saucer-shaped glass is used to serve cocktails that are meant to be sipped, such as a Champagne Cocktail. Much-debated folklore surrounds the glass's shape, rumored to have been shaped after Marie Antoinette's breast. It actually came about because of the use of coal in ovens after the ban of wood-burning stoves. The hotter ovens resulted in sturdier glasses that could hold the high-pressure bubbles without exploding. The coupe became a shorter type of goblet.

By using the correct glassware for each cocktail, you can elevate the drinking experience and add an extra touch of sophistication to your home bar.

## Glassware Tips

Beyond the obvious choice of putting Champagne in a flute and a Martini in its signature shape, choosing the right glassware is crucial in elevating the presentation and overall experience of a cocktail. Here are some tips to help you choose the right glassware:

***Purpose:*** Different drinks require different types of glassware. For example, martinis are traditionally served in a martini glass, while cocktails with crushed ice are served in tiki mugs.

***Capacity:*** Consider the amount of liquid your glassware will hold and choose glasses that are appropriate for the size of the drink you plan to serve.

*Material:* Glassware can be made from a variety of materials, including glass, crystal, and plastic. Choose a material that fits with the style and feel of your home bar.

*Budget:* Different materials have a wide range of costs. Decide whether you prefer to have a few nice pieces to showcase a few drinks or opt for less expensive options to give yourself a wider range of drink choices.

*Durability:* Consider the durability of the glassware you choose, especially if you plan on using it for entertaining guests.

*Style:* Glassware can be a great way to add a touch of style to your home bar. Choose glasses that complement your personal style and the overall aesthetic of your home.

By keeping these tips in mind, you can choose the right glassware to complement your home bar and enhance the presentation of your cocktails.

**Ice Bucket**

An ice bucket is an essential tool for any home bar setup. It is used to store ice and keep it cold for use in cocktails. The ice bucket typically has a handle for easy carrying and a lid to keep the ice from melting quickly. Ice buckets come in a variety of styles, materials, and sizes, and can be made of stainless steel, plastic, or other materials. The size of the ice bucket will depend on the amount of ice you need to store and the size of your bar. An ice bucket is an important tool for any home bartender, as it ensures that your cocktails will always have cold, fresh ice.

**Muddler**

A muddler is a bar tool that is used to crush or mix ingredients in a cocktail, such as fruits, herbs, and spices. It typically has a long, cylindrical shape with a flat or rounded end, which is used to crush ingredients in the bottom of a glass or shaker. Muddlers are an essential tool for making cocktails, as they help to release the flavors and aromas of ingredients and can also be used to dissolve sugar or other ingredients in the bottom of a glass. The use of a muddler has a long history in cocktail making and is still widely used today, especially in the preparation of cocktails such as Mojitos and Mint Juleps.

### Bar Towels

Bar towels are essential items in any home bar setup. They are used for cleaning up spills and wiping down the bar after use. They are usually made of cotton or microfiber and are soft, absorbent, and durable. The towels come in various sizes and can be folded or hung for easy access. Some bar towels even have a loop or hook for hanging them on a bar rail. It is important to have a good supply of bar towels on hand, as they help keep the bar area clean and hygienic.

### Ice Cube Trays

Ice cube trays are an essential part of any home bar setup. They are used to make ice cubes, which are crucial for chilling drinks and adding a touch of dilution to cocktails. Ice cube trays come in different shapes and sizes and can be made of plastic or silicone. Some trays even come with special features like snap-on lids to prevent spills or adjustable sizes to make different sizes of ice cubes. When choosing ice cube trays, it's important to look for trays that are durable, easy to clean, and produce ice cubes that are easy to remove. Investing in a good set of ice cube trays is a must for any at-home bartender.

### Alternative Ice Cubes

There are a few alternatives to regular ice cubes that are commonly used in bars and mixology. One alternative is circular ice cubes, which are larger and slower melting, making them ideal for drinks that need to be chilled without diluting the drink too quickly. Another alternative is metal ice cubes, which are made from stainless steel or other materials and are great for keeping drinks cold without diluting them. These alternative ice cubes can add an extra touch of elegance and sophistication to any cocktail and are a great addition to any home bar setup.

**Blender**

A blender is an essential piece of equipment for many cocktail recipes, particularly frozen drinks. The blender allows for ingredients to be blended smoothly, creating a creamy, frothy texture that is perfect for margaritas, daiquiris, and other frozen drinks. Blenders come in a variety of sizes and styles, with some being handheld and others being larger, countertop models. When choosing a blender for your home bar, consider factors such as power, speed, and durability. Some high-end models even come with pre-programmed settings specifically for making cocktails.

**Costs and Budgeting**

When setting up a home bar, it's important to consider the costs associated with stocking all the necessary equipment and ingredients. While there are many options available, it's essential to prioritize and budget accordingly. To determine what's essential, you'll want to consider the types of cocktails you want to make and the frequency with which you plan to make them. For example, if you are a big fan of frozen cocktails, then a blender would be an essential investment. On the other hand, if you are primarily making simple cocktails that don't require blending, then a blender may not be necessary.

When figuring out your budget, it's a good idea to start by investing in high-quality equipment that will last a long time, such as a well-made shaker, jigger, strainer, and bar spoon. High-quality glassware, like a set of coupes, highballs, and martini glasses, are also worth considering. While these items may be more expensive initially, they will last longer and be worth the investment in the long run.

Next, consider the ingredients you'll need to make your cocktails. Some of the most essential ingredients include spirits, bitters, syrups, and juices. If you're just starting out, it's a good idea to keep your ingredient list simple and focus on quality over quantity. As you become more confident in your mixology skills, you can start to experiment with a wider range of ingredients.

In terms of budgeting, it's important to remember that it's possible to start small and gradually build up your collection over time. By prioritizing quality over quantity and focusing on the essentials, you'll be able to create a well-stocked bar without breaking the bank.

**KEY TAKEAWAYS**

The key takeaways from this chapter are:

- A comprehensive understanding of the equipment required to set up a functional home bar, including shakers, strainers, jiggers, bar spoons, cutting boards, bottle openers, and more.
- Knowledge of the different types of glassware used in mixology, including martini glasses, old fashioned glasses, highball glasses, and more.
- Tips on how to choose the right glassware for each cocktail, based on its size, shape, and ingredients.
- An appreciation for the role of equipment and glassware in creating the perfect cocktail, and how it contributes to the overall mixology experience.

In the next chapter, we'll delve into the world of ingredients, breaking down the core spirits, liqueurs, wines, bitters, garnishes, and modifiers you'll need to stock your home bar. With this newfound knowledge, you'll be able to mix up classic cocktails with ease and start experimenting with your own unique creations. So, let's get ready to curate your arsenal of ingredients and take your home bar game to the next level!

# CHAPTER 3

# Curating your Arsenal of Ingredients

A bartender is only as good as their ingredients - it's time to arm yourself with the finest spirits, liqueurs, wines, bitters, garnishes, and modifiers. In Chapter four, we'll guide you on how to curate your own mixology arsenal and elevate your cocktail game to new heights.

In this chapter, we'll delve into the world of ingredients and explore the various core spirits, liquors, wines, bitters, garnishes, and modifiers that every home bartender should have in their arsenal. From the history and evolution of each ingredient to the best ways to store and use them, you'll gain a comprehensive understanding of the essential components that make up a classic cocktail. You'll learn the difference between different types of spirits, the role that bitters play in adding depth and flavor, and the importance of choosing the right garnishes to complement your drinks. By the end of this chapter, you'll have a solid foundation of knowledge on the ingredients that make up a well-stocked home bar and be ready to start experimenting with your own unique creations. Get ready to elevate your home bar game as we dive into the nitty-gritty details of curating your own ingredient collection.

In the world of mixology, ingredients are the building blocks of every classic cocktail. From the base spirits to the bitters, garnishes, and modifiers, each ingredient plays a crucial role in shaping the flavor, aroma, and overall experience of a drink.

## SPIRITS

Spirits, also known as distilled alcoholic beverages, are the backbone of any cocktail recipe. They are created by distilling fermented grains, fruits, or vegetables to increase the alcohol content and create a unique flavor profile. Some of the most common spirits used in mixology include vodka, gin, bourbon whiskey and Scotch whiskey, brandy, and rum. Each spirit has its own unique characteristics and can be used in a variety of cocktails to create depth and complexity. Now that you've learned some of the more popular ones used in classic drinks, let's delve deeper into each of these spirits, exploring their history, production methods, and flavor profiles to help you curate your own arsenal of ingredients.

*Vodka:* Vodka is a clear, odorless, and tasteless spirit that is made from either grain or potatoes. It is one of the most versatile and popular spirits in the world and is used in a variety of cocktails to create depth and complexity. Vodka has a rich history and was first produced in Eastern Europe in the 8th century. The production of vodka has evolved over time, and it is now made from a variety of grains and potatoes and is distilled multiple times to remove impurities and enhance its smoothness.

Vodka has a neutral flavor profile, making it a perfect base for cocktails that require the addition of other ingredients to add flavor. The production methods and ingredients used to make vodka can impact its unique characteristics and flavor profile. For example, vodka made from grain is typically considered to be smoother and have a slightly sweeter taste, while vodka made from potatoes is slightly more robust and have a creamier texture.

In cocktails, vodka can be used to balance other ingredients and provide a smooth, clean base for flavors to build upon. It can also be used to create cocktails with a clean and crisp taste, like the Classic Martini or the popular Cosmopolitan.

***Gin:*** Gin is a versatile and complex spirit that has a rich history and a wide range of flavor profiles. It is made from a neutral spirit that is flavored with botanicals, such as juniper berries, coriander, and angelica root. The exact blend of botanicals used in gin production is a closely guarded secret by each distillery, which leads to the wide variety of gin available on the market.

It can be traced back to the 17th century, when it was first produced in the Netherlands as a medicine. It quickly became popular as a beverage and was soon exported to England, where it gained widespread popularity. During the 18th and 19th centuries, gin became a staple of British culture, and many new gin styles were created, such as London Dry gin.

The unique characteristics of gin include its crisp and clean taste, which comes from the juniper berries, as well as its wide range of flavor profiles that are created by the different botanicals used in production. It is a versatile spirit that can be used in a variety of cocktails to create depth and complexity, making it a staple in any home bar.

This spirit is produced through a process of distillation, where the neutral spirit is flavored with botanicals. The botanicals are steeped in the spirit for a specified amount of time, and then distilled to create the final product. The type of still used, the botanicals used, and the length of steeping all play a role in the final flavor profile of the gin.

***Bourbon:*** Bourbon is a type of whiskey that is primarily made from corn, aged in charred oak barrels, and produced in the United States. It is known for its smooth and rich flavor profile, which is a result of the aging process and the interaction of the whiskey with the oak barrels. Bourbon has a long and storied history, with roots dating back to the late 1700s in the state of Kentucky.

The production is a carefully controlled process, with strict regulations in place to ensure the quality and authenticity of the spirit. The combination of at least 51%

corn, along with other grains like rye, wheat, and barley, gives bourbon its unique taste profile. The aging process can last anywhere from two to twenty years, with longer aging times resulting in a smoother and more complex flavor.

This oaky spirit can be used in a variety of cocktails to add depth and complexity to the drink. Its rich, smooth flavor profile makes it a popular choice for classic cocktails like the Old Fashioned and the Manhattan. Additionally, its versatility allows it to be paired with a range of ingredients, from sweet to bitter and everything in between.

**Brandy:** Brandy is a type of spirit made from distilled wine or fruit. This aging process gives brandy its unique character and flavor profile, which can range from smooth and fruity to bold and complex.

Brandy has a long and rich history, dating back to the 16th century. It originated in the Netherlands, where it was used as a medicinal drink to ward off illness. From there, it spread throughout Europe and eventually made its way to America. It's commonly made from grapes, but it can also be made from other fruits such as apples, peaches, and pears. The production process involves fermenting the fruit juice, distilling it, and then aging it in oak barrels. The aging process can range from several years to several decades, and this is what gives brandy its unique flavor profile. The longer it's aged, the more complex and nuanced the flavor becomes. Brandy has been a staple in classic cocktails such as the Sidecar, the Brandy Alexander, and the Cognac Flip.

The most popular types of brandy include Cognac and Armagnac, which are made from specific grapes and production methods. Brandy is also popular as an after-dinner drink, often sipped neat or on the rocks.

**Scotch:** Scotch is a type of whiskey that is distilled and aged in Scotland. It is made from malted barley, water, and yeast, and is typically aged for a minimum of three years in oak barrels. The unique characteristics of scotch include its smoky, peaty flavor profile, which is derived from the use of peat smoke to dry the malted barley. The production methods and aging process

used to make scotch also contribute to its distinct flavor, which can range from sweet and floral to bold and smoky. Scotch can be used in a variety of cocktails to add depth and complexity, and its strong flavor profile makes it a popular choice for sipping straight or on the rocks. The history of scotch dates back to the 15th century, and today it is considered one of the most refined and sought-after spirits in the world.

***Rum:*** Rum is a spirit that is made from sugarcane by-products, such as molasses or sugarcane juice, and then fermented and distilled. The unique characteristics of rum include its distinct flavor profiles, which range from sweet and caramel-like to spicy and bold.

There are two main types of rum production methods: continuous distillation and pot still distillation. Continuous distillation is a more efficient method, where the sugarcane by-products are continuously fed into the still and the rum is produced in a continuous flow. Pot still distillation, on the other hand, is a more traditional method where the sugarcane by-products are fermented in a large pot and then distilled in smaller batches.

The type of rum produced depends on the production method used and the location of the distillery. For example, lighter rums are often produced using continuous distillation, while more robust and flavorful rums are produced using pot still distillation. The aging process also plays a significant role in the flavor profile of rum. Rums are aged in oak barrels, which can be charred or uncharred, and the length of aging and the type of barrel used can greatly impact the final flavor of the rum.

## BITTERS

Bitters are a key ingredient in mixology, adding a unique flavor profile and complexity to cocktails. Unlike other mixers, bitters are highly concentrated and typically used in small amounts to enhance the overall taste of a drink. They can range from sweet and floral to bitter and herbal and can be made from a variety of ingredients such as roots, bark, fruits, and spices.

Some of the most common bitters used in mixology include Angostura bitters, Peychaud's bitters, orange bitters, and aromatic bitters. These ingredients are made by steeping a variety of herbs, spices, roots, and other botanicals in high-proof alcohol to create a concentrated, flavorful liquid. Bitters are typically added in small amounts to cocktails to enhance the overall flavor profile and balance the sweetness, acidity, and bitterness in the drink.

## LIQUEURS

Liqueurs are sweet, flavored alcoholic beverages that are typically enjoyed as after-dinner drinks or used as mixers in cocktails. They are made by infusing spirits with sugar and flavorings, which can include fruit, spices, nuts, and other ingredients. Unlike spirits, which are usually clear and have a high alcohol content, liqueurs are often brightly colored and have a lower alcohol content, usually around 15-30%. Some popular liqueurs include triple sec, amaretto, Bailey's Irish Cream, and Kahlua. In mixology, liqueurs are used to add sweetness, flavor, and balance to cocktails, and they can also be used as a base for making other ingredients, such as syrups.

The unique characteristics of liqueurs are their sweetness, syrupy texture, and intense flavors, which can range from fruit-based to nutty, chocolatey, and even herbal.

The history of liqueurs dates back to medieval times, when they were initially made as medicinal remedies. Today, liqueurs are used in a variety of cocktails to add flavor, balance, and sweetness. They are produced using a combination of distilled spirits, flavorings, and sweeteners, which are then blended to create the final product.

Production methods of liqueurs vary depending on the brand and the specific type of liqueur. Some liqueurs are made by infusing spirits with natural ingredients such as fruits, nuts, spices, and herbs, while others are created using artificial flavorings and sweeteners. The production process can also involve distillation, filtration, and aging, which can impact the final flavor profile of the liqueur. Common liqueurs used in mixology include triple sec, Cointreau, Grand Marnier (citrus-based), Drambuie, Baileys (nutty), Campari, Aperol (bitter). These liqueurs can add depth and complexity to cocktails and are essential ingredients in many classic and contemporary drinks.

## WINES

Wine is a crucial component in the world of mixology. From sweet, fruity wines to dry, crisp wines, each type of wine brings its own unique flavor profile to the table. In cocktails, wines can be used as the base or as a modifier to add depth and complexity to the drink. The most popular types of wine used in mixology include fortified wines, such as Vermouth and Sherry, as well as sparkling wines, such as Champagne and Prosecco.

Wines are a popular ingredient in cocktails, adding depth and complexity to a drink. There are a variety of wine types, each with its own unique characteristics, production methods, and flavor profiles.

Wines are made by fermenting grapes or other fruit. The process of winemaking has a long and rich history, dating back thousands of years to ancient civilizations. Today, winemaking techniques have evolved and become more sophisticated, resulting in a wide range of wine styles and flavor profiles.

Wines can be used in a variety of cocktails to create depth and complexity. For example, red wine can be used to add a rich, fruity flavor to a cocktail, while white wine can provide a crisp, refreshing taste. Sparkling wines, such as Champagne, can add a festive touch to a cocktail and can be used to create sparkling drinks.

When selecting wines for use in cocktails, it's important to choose a wine that complements the other ingredients in the drink. For example, a sweet wine may not work well in a cocktail that contains bitter ingredients, while a dry wine may be too harsh in a drink that is meant to be sweet.

Wines can help to elevate a cocktail to a new level of sophistication and complexity.

## GARNISHES

Garnishes are the finishing touches to a cocktail that not only enhance the visual appeal but also add flavor and aroma to the drink. They can range from simple twists of citrus peel to elaborate fruit and herb arrangements. Some popular garnishes include lemon or lime wedges, orange slices, cherries, olives, and fresh herbs like mint or basil. The right garnish can elevate a drink to a whole new level and bring out the flavors and aromas of the ingredients in the cocktail. When selecting garnishes, it's important to consider the flavors and aromas of the ingredients in the drink and choose garnishes that complement or enhance those flavors.

The history of garnishes dates back to the earliest days of cocktail making when bartenders first began to experiment with different ways to add flavor and aroma to their drinks. Over time, the use of garnishes evolved, with bartenders seeking out new and innovative ways to add visual appeal to their cocktails. Today, garnishes are an integral part of the mixology process, with bartenders using them to add a touch of sophistication and style to their creations.

When it comes to production methods, garnishes are typically hand-selected and prepared by bartenders or mixologists, who take care to choose the freshest and highest quality ingredients. The flavor profiles of garnishes can vary greatly, depending on the type of fruit, herb, or other ingredient used. Some garnishes are tart and acidic, while others are sweet and fruity, and still others are spicy or herbal. When used correctly, garnishes can help to bring balance to a cocktail, and can add depth and complexity to the overall flavor profile.

## MODIFIERS

Modifiers are ingredients added to cocktails to enhance the flavor and balance of the drink. These ingredients are added in small quantities to a cocktail, usually in the form of a splash or a few dashes, to help bring out the flavors of the other ingredients. When used correctly, modifiers can help take a cocktail from good to great, elevating the overall taste and experience of the drink.

Modifiers are ingredients added to cocktails to enhance and alter the flavor profile of the drink. These ingredients are often syrups, juices, or liqueurs that add sweetness, acidity, or additional flavor notes to a cocktail. The unique characteristics of modifiers are their versatility and ability to balance and enhance the flavors of a cocktail.

Modifiers have a rich history in mixology, dating back to the earliest days of cocktail culture. Originally, simple syrups were used to add sweetness to cocktails, but as the art of mixology evolved, the use of modifiers expanded to include a wide range of ingredients. Today, mixologists continue to experiment with new and innovative modifiers to create unique and complex flavor profiles.

Production methods for modifiers can vary, but many are made by combining ingredients such as sugar, water, and flavorings, and then boiling and reducing the mixture to create a syrup or concentrate. Some modifiers, such as juices, are simply extracted from fruits and vegetables, while others, like liqueurs, are made by infusing spirits with flavorings and sweeteners.

Common modifiers include simple syrups, grenadine, orgeat, triple sec, and various fruit juices. The use of modifiers in cocktails allows mixologists to add depth and complexity to their creations, making them truly unique and memorable experiences.

**KEY TAKEAWAYS**

In this chapter, we delved into the essential ingredients that make up the backbone of any great cocktail. From spirits and bitters, to garnishes and modifiers, we explored the unique characteristics and history of each, and how they can be used to add depth and complexity to your drinks.
The key takeaways from this chapter included:

- Understanding the different categories of ingredients used in mixology, including spirits, bitters, liqueurs, wines, garnishes, and modifiers.
- Knowledge of the unique characteristics of each type of ingredient, including their history, production methods, and flavor profiles, which can help you to create depth and complexity in your cocktails.
- An appreciation for the role that each ingredient plays in the overall taste and experience of a cocktail, and the importance of carefully selecting and balancing ingredients for the best results.
- A deeper understanding of how to create a well-stocked home bar, with the right ingredients and tools to make a variety of classic and original cocktails.

With a comprehensive understanding of the ingredients and equipment needed to create classic cocktails, it's time to turn our attention to the art of mixing and creating. In the next chapter, we'll delve into the techniques and methods used to bring these timeless drinks to life. From muddling to shaking, stirring to straining, you'll learn all the essential skills to become a master mixologist in your own home. So, let's get ready to start mixing!

# CHAPTER 4
## Techniques & Methods

Discover the art and science behind the perfect cocktail as we unveil the essential techniques and methods that have transformed ordinary drinks into timeless classics. Are you ready to master the secrets of mixology?

Now that you're equipped with the essential tools and glassware for your home bar, it's time to explore the various techniques and methods used in mixology. From shaking and stirring to muddling and layering, these techniques will elevate your cocktail-making skills and help you craft delicious drinks with confidence. In this chapter, we'll cover the following techniques in detail:

- Shaking
- Stirring
- Muddling
- Layering
- Straining
- Garnishing
- Flaming
- Serving

## Shaking

Shaking is one of the fundamental techniques in mixology. Used to quickly chill and dilute cocktails while adding air for a frothy texture, shaking is a great choice when creating cocktails with fruit juices, syrups, or any other ingredients that need to be thoroughly combined.

To properly shake a cocktail, you'll need all your ingredients and ice. Every drink requires different times of shaking to achieve its ideal consistency and temperature.

Shaken-Up (10-15 seconds, depending on intensity of shaking): These cocktails require vigorous shaking to mix ingredients thoroughly and achieve an airy and balanced result. Shake times vary according to recipe and desired result - for instance if making classic Daiquiris this should typically involve 10-15 second shakes to properly integrate rum, lime juice and simple syrup for optimal results - the goal being an integrated and harmonious cocktail experience.

Shaken Down on Cubed Ice (5-8 seconds): This method can be useful when beverages require only minimal shaking time but still benefit from some chilling and diluting. Cubed ice provides moderate diluting properties while maintaining smooth texture. One example of such an application would be shaking down a whiskey Sour for approximately 8-8 seconds in order to combine its whiskey, lemon juice, and simple syrup into an enjoyable cocktail that meets both chilling and diluting requirements.

Shaken-Down on Crushed Ice (5 seconds): When shaken-down on crushed ice, shake times tend to be shorter as smaller ice particles provide faster cooling and diluting effects. This method is ideal for drinks such as the Mint Julep which require rapid chilling such as its constituent components bourbon, sugar, fresh mint leaves before serving over crushed ice.

Dry Shaking is an indispensable method used for creating cocktails featuring ingredients such as egg whites, cream and other emulsifiers. This process involves initially shaking ingredients without adding ice before gradually adding pieces to create a foamy texture before finally adding colder ice and shaking again for chilling purposes. Dry shaking serves to properly emulsify and aerate ingredients for maximum creamy velvety textures, as well as adding air for visual interest to form visually attractive foam or froth on top of drinks. Dry shaking is often utilized in cocktails such as the Whiskey Sour or Ramos Gin Fizz where egg white needs to be fully mixed into the drink. After this stage of dry shaking has been completed, ice is added and shaken again in order to chill and dilute it further before straining into a glass for serving.

## Stirring

Stirring is a gentler technique than shaking and is used for cocktails that contain only spirits or liqueurs. The goal is to chill and dilute the drink without incorporating air, resulting in a silky, crystal-clear texture.

To stir a cocktail, add all your ingredients and ice to a mixing glass. Using a bar spoon, gently stir the mixture for about 20-30 seconds, making sure the spoon glides smoothly around the glass. Once the drink is well mixed, strain it into the desired glass, and serve.

## Muddling

Muddling involves crushing ingredients like fruit, herbs, or sugar cubes to release their flavors and oils into a cocktail. This technique is commonly used in drinks like Mojitos and Old Fashioneds.

To muddle, place the ingredients in the bottom of a sturdy glass or shaker. Use a muddler to press and crush the ingredients gently, being careful not to over-muddle, which can result in bitter flavors. Once the ingredients are sufficiently crushed, add the remaining components of the cocktail, and mix as needed.

## Layering

Layering is an advanced technique used to create visually appealing cocktails with distinct layers of color and flavor. This method relies on the specific gravity of each ingredient, which determines how they will layer in the glass.

To layer a cocktail, slowly pour each ingredient over the back of a bar spoon, starting with the heaviest ingredient and working your way up to the lightest. Hold the spoon against the inside of the glass at a slight angle to ensure a smooth pour. Be patient, and practice to perfect this technique.

## Straining

Straining is used to separate the liquid from the ice and other solid ingredients in a cocktail. The most common strainers are the Hawthorne strainer and the Julep strainer. To strain a cocktail, simply hold the strainer over the shaker or mixing glass and pour the liquid into the serving glass.

## Garnishing

Garnishing is the final touch that adds visual appeal and extra flavor to your cocktail. Common garnishes include citrus twists, fruit slices, herbs, and olives. To garnish your cocktail, choose a garnish that complements the flavors of the drink and adds a touch of visual interest.

## Flaming

Flaming is where a spirit or liqueur is briefly ignited before being added to the drink in order to create a smokey or caramelized flavor. This can add a strong sense of visual representation to the drink and is typically done by pouring the alcohol into a warm, shallow dish, igniting it with a flame, and then quickly pouring it into the cocktail while the flames are still burning.

## Serving Up

A "cocktail "up" involves straining it directly into a stemmed glass without adding ice for optimal sipping experience. This technique is popularly employed with classic cocktails like martinis and cosmopolitans; by serving it this way you can appreciate all its flavors without melting ice diluting its aromas; creating a refined and pleasurable drinking experience.

## Serving Down

Another method for serving cocktails "down" involves pouring them over fresh ice cubes in either a lowball glass or rocks glass and refrigerating. This presentation works particularly well when your drink benefits from some degree of diluting and cooler temperature; drinks like Old Fashioneds or Negronis often benefit from being presented this way as this allows the flavors to develop over time as the ice gradually melts, providing an opportunity to mellow and evolve further as each sip slowly dissipation process.

**Serving Neat**

"Neat" refers to serving spirits such as whiskey or brandy at room temperature without adding additional ingredients, like ice, in order to best appreciate its character and complexity without any external flavors diluting its essence. Neat servings often come with an accompanying glass of water to cleanse the palate between sips.

Mastering these fundamental techniques and methods will significantly improve your mixology skills and allow you to create cocktails with finesse and flair. Practice each technique to develop your own style and build confidence behind the bar. With these skills in your arsenal, you're well on your way to becoming an accomplished home bartender.

## TECHNIQUE HISTORY

Let's dive into the history and knowledge behind various techniques and methods used in creating cocktails. Understanding the origins and purposes of these methods will not only enhance your mixology skills but also give you a greater appreciation for the craftsmanship involved in crafting the perfect cocktail.

***Shaking:*** Shaking is one of the most iconic techniques in mixology, dating back to the 19th century. The first recorded use of a cocktail shaker was in 1848 when a bartender in the United States combined a glass and a tin cup to create a makeshift shaker. Shaking is used to mix, chill, and aerate cocktails quickly. This method is particularly effective for drinks containing fruit juices, dairy, or egg whites, as it helps to create a frothy texture and a well-integrated mix of ingredients.

***Stirring:*** Stirring is a more delicate and controlled technique compared to shaking. It's used for cocktails that are composed mainly of spirits, like a Martini or a Manhattan. Stirring is an older method than shaking and can be traced back to the early 1800s. It's ideal for combining ingredients without overly diluting or aerating the drink, preserving the clarity and smooth texture of spirit-forward cocktails.

*Muddling:* Muddling is a technique used to extract flavors from fresh ingredients, such as fruits, herbs, and spices. The origins of muddling can be traced back to the classic Mint Julep, a cocktail that dates back to the 18th century. By gently crushing the ingredients with a muddler, you release their essential oils and flavors, which then blend with the other components of the drink.

*Building:* The building technique involves layering ingredients directly into the glass in which the cocktail will be served. This method is commonly used for simple, low-alcohol drinks like the Collins or the Mojito. Building a cocktail allows the individual flavors of each ingredient to shine through while still creating a harmonious blend.

*Straining:* Straining is a technique used to separate liquid from solid ingredients, such as ice or fruit pulp. The Hawthorne strainer, invented in the late 19th century, is the most common type of strainer used in cocktail making. Straining ensures that your cocktail is free of unwanted solids, and it also helps to control the dilution of the drink by removing excess ice.

*Garnishing:* The art of garnishing has been an essential part of cocktail presentation since the early days of mixology. Garnishes serve multiple purposes, including adding visual appeal, enhancing the aroma, and providing additional flavor elements. Some of the most iconic garnishes include the olive in a Martini, the cherry in a Manhattan, and the citrus twist in a Negroni.

*Flaming:* Flaming, or setting a cocktail on fire, is a dramatic technique used to enhance the flavor and aroma of a drink. Its history dates back to the 19th century, with the Blue Blazer being one of the earliest known flaming cocktails. The flames caramelize sugars, add smoky flavors, and create an unforgettable presentation.

By understanding the history and purpose behind these techniques and methods, you'll be better equipped to craft cocktails with precision and care. Each technique has its own unique purpose and effect on a cocktail's flavor, texture, and presentation. Mastering these methods will not only elevate your mixology skills but also give you a deeper appreciation for the art of creating classic cocktails.

## A TALL DRINK OF HISTORY

We've explored various techniques and methods used in mixology, from shaking and stirring to muddling and garnishing. To further illustrate the importance of these techniques, let's take a closer look at a classic cocktail and the role these methods play in its creation: the Old Fashioned.

The Old Fashioned has a rich history, dating back to the early 1800s. It is said to have originated in Louisville, Kentucky, at a private social club called the Pendennis Club. The recipe was later brought to the Waldorf-Astoria Hotel in New York City, where it gained widespread popularity.

The Old Fashioned is a perfect example of how different mixology techniques come together to create a timeless and well-balanced cocktail. Here's a breakdown of how these techniques are used in the making of this classic drink:

*Muddling:* The Old Fashioned begins with muddling a sugar cube, bitters, and a splash of water in the bottom of a glass. This technique releases the flavors of the sugar and bitters, creating a flavorful base for the cocktail.

*Building:* Once the sugar and bitters have been muddled, the drink is built by adding ice and whiskey to the glass. This technique allows the individual flavors of the whiskey and the muddled ingredients to blend together while still maintaining their distinct characteristics.

*Stirring:* After the whiskey is added, the drink is stirred gently to integrate the flavors and chill the cocktail. Stirring is a more delicate method than shaking, which helps preserve the smooth texture and clarity of the drink.

*Garnishing:* The Old Fashioned is traditionally garnished with a twist of citrus peel, usually orange or lemon. The oils from the citrus peel enhance the aroma of the drink and add a subtle layer of flavor.

The story of the Old Fashioned showcases the importance of mixology techniques in creating a classic cocktail. Each method plays a crucial role in building the drink's unique flavor profile, texture, and presentation. By understanding and mastering these techniques, you'll be able to appreciate the craftsmanship involved in creating timeless cocktails and elevate your own mixology skills.

**KEY TAKEAWAYS**

The key takeaways from this chapter include:

- Understanding the importance of various mixology techniques and how they impact the final outcome of your cocktails.
- Learning when to use specific techniques, such as shaking for cocktails with fruit juices or syrups and stirring for spirit-only drinks.
- Mastering the art of muddling to release flavors from ingredients like fruit and herbs without over-muddling and creating bitter flavors.
- Perfecting the layering technique to create visually appealing cocktails with distinct layers of color and flavor.
- Utilizing straining methods to separate liquid from ice and solid ingredients, ensuring a smooth and enjoyable drinking experience.
- Enhancing the presentation and flavor of your cocktails with thoughtful and complementary garnishes, or using the technique of flaming.

With a solid understanding of these techniques and methods, you're now prepared to tackle the world of mixology with confidence. As you progress, you'll develop your own unique style and approach to crafting cocktails, impressing your friends and family with your newfound skills.

In the upcoming chapters, we'll dive deeper into the art of mixology by exploring various cocktail recipes and learning how to mix light and dark spirits. We'll also delve into the creative process of infusing classic cocktails with unique twists, allowing you to develop your own signature drinks. So, get ready to put your skills to the test and embark on a journey to become a master home bartender!

# CHAPTER 5
## The Rules to Mixology

Ever wonder why some cocktails taste divine while others fall flat? Unravel the ten golden rules of mixology that will elevate your cocktail-making skills from ordinary to extraordinary.

As you continue your journey to becoming an accomplished home bartender, it's essential to understand the guiding principles that underpin the art of mixology. These rules will serve as a foundation for your cocktail-making endeavors, ensuring consistent and delicious results every time. In this chapter, we'll outline the key rules to follow when crafting cocktails, including:

- Balance
- Freshness
- Quality ingredients
- Ice matters
- Know your audience
- Practice and experimentation
- Pay attention to dilution
- Experiment with balance
- Keep your bar and tools clean

## Balance

Balance is the cornerstone of great mixology. A well-balanced cocktail harmonizes its ingredients, ensuring that no single flavor overpowers the others. To achieve balance, consider the sweetness, acidity, bitterness, and alcohol content of your cocktails. Use simple syrup, fruit juices, and liqueurs to balance acidity, and bitters to counteract sweetness. Adjust your recipes to suit your taste and aim for a harmonious blend of flavors.

## Freshness

Fresh ingredients can make all the difference in your cocktails. Whenever possible, opt for fresh fruit juices, herbs, and garnishes. Fresh ingredients have a more vibrant flavor and will elevate the taste of your drinks. Also, freshly squeezed fruit juices are far superior to store-bought options in terms of flavor and quality. Freshly squeezed citrus juice, for example, has a brightness and complexity that can't be matched by store-bought alternatives. Similarly, using fresh herbs like mint or basil can elevate your drinks and impart vibrant flavors.

## Quality ingredients

Investing in quality ingredients is crucial to creating exceptional cocktails. Choose high-quality spirits, liqueurs, and mixers to ensure the best possible flavor in your drinks. While it's not always necessary to buy the most expensive options, avoid the cheapest ingredients, as they may negatively impact the taste of your cocktails.

## Ice matters

The quality and quantity of ice used in your cocktails can significantly affect the outcome. Use large, clear ice cubes or spheres for stirred and built cocktails, as they melt more slowly and provide consistent chilling and dilution. For shaken cocktails, use smaller, regular ice cubes for rapid cooling and dilution. Remember to always use fresh, clean ice to avoid introducing unwanted flavors to your drinks.

### Know your audience

Catering to the tastes and preferences of your guests is a key aspect of successful home bartending. Be familiar with the likes and dislikes of your audience and adjust your cocktails accordingly. If you're entertaining a group with diverse tastes, consider offering a selection of cocktails that cater to different preferences, such as light and refreshing, spirit-forward, or fruity and sweet options.

### Practice and experimentation

As with any skill, practice and experimentation are crucial to mastering mixology. Don't be afraid to try new recipes, techniques, and ingredients. Learn from your mistakes and continue refining your skills. Embrace creativity and develop your own unique style, as this will set your cocktails apart and make them memorable.

### Pay attention to dilution

Dilution is an essential aspect of creating balanced cocktails. Too little dilution can lead to a strong, overpowering drink, while too much can result in a weak, watery cocktail. Shaking or stirring a cocktail with ice helps to achieve the right level of dilution.

### Experiment with balance

Balance is crucial in mixology. A well-balanced cocktail has the right harmony between sweet, sour, bitter, and alcoholic flavors. Don't be afraid to experiment with different ratios and ingredient combinations to find the perfect balance for your taste preferences.

### Keep your bar and tools clean

A clean workspace is vital for maintaining the quality and presentation of your cocktails. Make sure to clean your tools and bar area regularly, and always use clean glassware for serving drinks.

**WHY RULES MATTER**

Understanding and abiding by these ten rules is essential for several reasons:

- They ensure a consistent and high-quality experience for you and your guests. Following these rules will help you create delicious, well-balanced cocktails that everyone can enjoy.
- The rules help maintain proper hygiene and cleanliness. Keeping your workspace and tools clean not only improves the overall cocktail-making experience but also ensures the safety and health of your guests.
- These rules encourage creativity and experimentation. Mixology is an art form that allows for endless possibilities. By understanding the basics and pushing your limits, you can discover new flavor combinations and techniques that make your cocktails stand out.
- Adhering to these rules helps you gain confidence in your mixology skills. The more you practice and understand the principles of mixology, the more competent and comfortable you'll become in creating and serving cocktails.
- The rules serve as a foundation for building your knowledge and expertise. By mastering these fundamental principles, you can continue to expand your skills and delve deeper into the world of mixology.
- By following these ten rules, you'll be well on your way to becoming a skilled mixologist capable of crafting exceptional cocktails and providing a memorable experience for your friends, family, and guests.

**A HISTORY OF RULES**

In Chapter 5, we discussed the importance of following a set of rules to create well-balanced and delicious cocktails. To further emphasize the significance of these rules, let's look at the story of Ada Coleman, a groundbreaking female bartender who adhered to mixology principles and became a legend in the industry.

Ada Coleman, often referred to as "Coley," began her bartending career in the early 1900s at Claridge's Hotel in London. In 1903, she was appointed the head bartender at the prestigious Savoy Hotel's American Bar, becoming one of the first female bartenders in a male-dominated industry.

Coleman was known for her meticulous attention to detail, adherence to mixology rules, and her warm, welcoming demeanor. Her dedication to following mixology principles, such as using fresh ingredients, balancing flavors, and measuring accurately, allowed her to create exquisite and memorable cocktails.

One of her most famous creations was the Hanky Panky, a cocktail that perfectly demonstrates her dedication to the rules of mixology. The Hanky Panky is a well-balanced blend of gin, sweet vermouth, and Fernet-Branca and garnished with an orange twist. This cocktail showcases Coleman's understanding of balancing flavors, using quality ingredients, and proper garnishing techniques.

Coleman's commitment to mixology rules and her innovative spirit helped her achieve great success as a bartender, and she went on to mentor future generations of bartenders, including Harry Craddock, who would later write the renowned Savoy Cocktail Book. Her dedication to her craft left a lasting impact on the industry and paved the way for other women in the field.

The story of Ada Coleman illustrates the importance of adhering to mixology rules and principles. By following these guidelines, she was able to create exceptional cocktails, excel in her profession, and leave a lasting legacy in the world of mixology.

**KEY TAKEAWAYS**

By adhering to these fundamental rules of mixology, you'll be well on your way to crafting consistently delicious and well-balanced cocktails. Keep these principles in mind as you continue to hone your skills:

- Strive for balance in your cocktails, considering the interplay of sweetness, acidity, bitterness, and alcohol content.
- Prioritize freshness by using fresh fruit juices, herbs, and garnishes whenever possible.
- Invest in quality ingredients, including spirits, liqueurs, and mixers, to ensure the best possible flavor in your drinks.
- Recognize the importance of ice in both chilling and diluting your cocktails, and use the appropriate ice for each drink.

- Cater to your audience's tastes and preferences, and offer a variety of cocktail options to suit different palates.
- Continuously practice and experiment with new recipes, techniques, and ingredients to refine your skills and develop your own unique style.

As you progress through the following chapters, these rules will serve as a foundation for your mixology endeavors. Keep them in mind as you explore various cocktail recipes, learn how to mix different types of spirits, and experiment with unique flavor combinations.

In Chapter 6, we'll dive into the art of mixing light spirits, including vodka, gin, white rum, and white wine. You'll discover a range of delicious recipes and learn how to showcase the delicate and refreshing characteristics of these spirits in your cocktails.

Following that, in Chapter 7, we'll explore the world of dark spirits, such as whiskey, bourbon, brandy, dark rum, and red wine. You'll learn how to create rich, complex, and satisfying cocktails that highlight the depth and warmth of these darker spirits.

Finally, in Chapter 8, we'll delve into the creative process of infusing classic cocktails with unique twists, allowing you to put your own personal stamp on time-honored recipes. This chapter will provide inspiration for taking your mixology skills to new heights and developing your own signature drinks.

By adhering to the rules outlined in this chapter and continuing to practice and experiment, you'll be well on your way to becoming a skilled and confident home bartender. Your friends and family will be impressed by your newfound expertise, and you'll have the satisfaction of creating memorable and delicious cocktails for any occasion. So, let's continue on this exciting journey and unlock the full potential of your home bar!

## A SHORT MESSAGE FROM THE AUTHOR

Hey, are you enjoying the book? I'd love to hear your thoughts!

Many readers do not know how hard reviews are to come by, and how much they help an author.

I would be incredibly grateful if you could take just 60 seconds to write a brief review on Amazon, even if it's just a few sentences!

>> Click here to leave a quick review

Thank you for taking the time to share your thoughts!

Your review will genuinely make a difference for me and help gain exposure for my work.

Whiskey Morgan

# CHAPTER 6

## Mixing Light Spirits

Ever wondered why some cocktails taste divine while others fall flat? Unravel the ten golden rules of mixology that will elevate your cocktail-making skills from ordinary to extraordinary.

In this chapter, we'll explore the world of light spirits, including vodka, gin, white rum, and white wine. These spirits are characterized by their clear color and generally lighter, more refreshing flavors. You'll discover a range of delicious cocktail recipes that showcase the unique characteristics of each spirit, allowing you to create versatile and crowd-pleasing drinks for any occasion.

**VODKA**

Vodka is a neutral spirit, known for its clean taste and versatility in cocktails. It provides a smooth and subtle base that allows other flavors to shine. Here are five vodka-based cocktails to try:

## VODKA MARTINI

A classic, elegant cocktail made with vodka and dry vermouth, garnished with a lemon twist or olives.

Ingredients:
- 2 oz vodka
- 1/2 oz dry vermouth
- Lemon twist or olives, for garnish
- Ice, for stirring and serving

Instructions:
1. Fill a mixing glass with ice cubes.
2. Add 2 oz of vodka and 1/2 oz of dry vermouth to the mixing glass.
3. Stir the mixture with a bar spoon for 20-30 seconds until well-chilled.
4. Strain the mixture into a chilled martini glass.
5. Garnish the cocktail with a lemon twist or olives.

## MOSCOW MULE

A refreshing mix of vodka, ginger beer, and fresh lime juice, served in a copper mug.

Ingredients:
- 2 oz vodka
- 4 oz ginger beer
- 1/2 oz fresh lime juice
- Lime wedge, for garnish
- Ice, for serving
- Copper mug, for serving

Instructions:
1. Fill a copper mug with ice cubes.
2. Add 2 oz of vodka, 4 oz of ginger beer, and 1/2 oz of fresh lime juice to the copper mug.
3. Stir the mixture with a bar spoon.
4. Garnish the cocktail with a lime wedge.

## COSMOPOLITAN

A sophisticated blend of vodka, orange liqueur, cranberry juice, and fresh lime juice.

Ingredients:

- 1 1/2 oz vodka
- 1/2 oz orange liqueur (Cointreau or triple sec)
- 1 oz cranberry juice
- 1/2 oz fresh lime juice
- Lime twist or orange peel, for garnish
- Ice, for shaking and serving

Instructions:

1. Fill a shaker with ice cubes.
2. Add 1 1/2 oz of vodka, 1/2 oz of orange liqueur, 1 oz of cranberry juice, and 1/2 oz of fresh lime juice to the shaker.
3. Shake the mixture vigorously for 10-15 seconds.
4. Strain the mixture into a chilled martini glass.
5. Garnish the cocktail with a lime twist or orange peel.

## BLOODY MARY

A savory combination of vodka, tomato juice, Worcestershire sauce, hot sauce, and various spices, garnished with celery, olives, or pickles.

Ingredients:
- 1 1/2 oz vodka
- 3 oz tomato juice
- 1/2 oz lemon juice
- 2 dashes Worcestershire sauce
- 2 dashes hot sauce (such as Tabasco)
- Pinch of ground black pepper
- Pinch of smoked paprika or regular paprika
- Pinch of horseradish (optional)
- Celery stalk, olives, or pickles, for garnish
- Ice, for shaking and serving

Instructions:
1. Fill a shaker with ice cubes.
2. Add 1 1/2 oz of vodka, 3 oz of tomato juice, 1/2 oz of lemon juice, 2 dashes of Worcestershire sauce, 2 dashes of hot sauce, a pinch of ground black pepper, and a pinch of smoked paprika to the shaker.
3. If desired, add a pinch of horseradish to the shaker.
4. Shake the mixture vigorously for 10-15 seconds.
5. Strain the mixture into a highball glass filled with ice.
6. Garnish the cocktail with a celery stalk, olives, or pickles.

### LEMON DROP

A sweet and tangy mix of vodka, triple sec, simple syrup, and fresh lemon juice, served in a sugar-rimmed glass.

Ingredients:
- 2 oz vodka
- 1/2 oz triple sec
- 1 oz simple syrup
- 1 oz fresh lemon juice
- Sugar, for rimming the glass
- Lemon wheel, for garnish
- Ice, for shaking and serving

Instructions:
1. Rim a chilled martini glass with sugar.
2. Fill a shaker with ice cubes.
3. Add 2 oz of vodka, 1/2 oz of triple sec, 1 oz of simple syrup, and 1 oz of fresh lemon juice to the shaker.
4. Shake the mixture vigorously for 10-15 seconds.
5. Strain the mixture into the sugar-rimmed martini glass.
6. Garnish the cocktail with a lemon wheel.

## GIN

Gin is a spirit flavored with juniper berries and various botanicals, giving it a distinctive and complex flavor profile. Its herbal and floral notes make it a popular choice for refreshing, aromatic cocktails. Here are five gin-based cocktails to try:

### GIN & TONIC

A timeless and simple combination of gin and tonic water, garnished with a lime or lemon wedge.

Ingredients:

- 2 oz gin
- Tonic water, to top
- Lime or lemon wedge, for garnish
- Ice, for serving

Instructions:

1. Fill a highball glass with ice cubes.
2. Add 2 oz of gin to the glass.
3. Top with tonic water.
4. Stir the mixture gently.
5. Garnish the cocktail with a lime or lemon wedge.

## NEGRONI

A bold, bitter cocktail made with equal parts gin, Campari, and sweet vermouth, garnished with an orange peel.

Ingredients:
- 1 oz gin
- 1 oz Campari
- 1 oz sweet vermouth
- Orange peel, for garnish
- Ice, for stirring and serving

Instructions:
1. Fill a mixing glass with ice cubes.
2. Add 1 oz of gin, 1 oz of Campari, and 1 oz of sweet vermouth to the mixing glass.
3. Stir the mixture with a bar spoon for 20-30 seconds until well-chilled.
4. Strain the mixture into a chilled rocks glass filled with ice.
5. Garnish the cocktail with an orange peel.

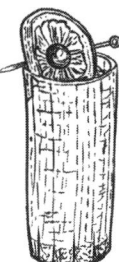

## TOM COLLINS

A classic mix of gin, lemon juice, simple syrup, and soda water, garnished with a lemon wheel and cherry.

Ingredients:

- 2 oz gin
- 1 oz lemon juice
- 1/2 oz simple syrup
- Soda water, to top
- Lemon wheel and cherry, for garnish
- Ice, for serving

Instructions:

1. Fill a Collins glass with ice cubes.
2. Add 2 oz of gin, 1 oz of lemon juice, and 1/2 oz of simple syrup to the glass.
3. Stir the mixture gently.
4. Top with soda water.
5. Garnish the cocktail with a lemon wheel and cherry.

## GIMLET

A tart and tangy blend of gin and lime juice, sweetened with simple syrup.

Ingredients:
- 2 oz gin
- 1 oz lime juice
- 1/2 oz simple syrup
- Ice, for shaking and serving

Instructions:
1. Fill a shaker with ice cubes.
2. Add 2 oz of gin, 1 oz of lime juice, and 1/2 oz of simple syrup to the shaker.
3. Shake the mixture vigorously for 10-15 seconds.
4. Strain the mixture into a chilled martini glass.
5. Garnish the cocktail with a lime wheel or wedge.

## FRENCH 75

A sophisticated concoction of gin, lemon juice, simple syrup, and Champagne, garnished with a lemon twist.

Ingredients:
- 1 1/2 oz gin
- 1/2 oz lemon juice
- 1/2 oz simple syrup
- Champagne, to top
- Lemon twist, for garnish
- Ice, for shaking

Instructions:
1. Fill a shaker with ice cubes.
2. Add 1 1/2 oz of gin, 1/2 oz of lemon juice, and 1/2 oz of simple syrup to the shaker.
3. Shake the mixture vigorously for 10-15 seconds.
4. Strain the mixture into a chilled Champagne flute.
5. Top with Champagne.
6. Garnish the cocktail with a lemon twist.

## WHITE RUM

White rum is a light, slightly sweet spirit distilled from sugarcane or molasses. Its subtle flavor makes it an ideal base for a variety of tropical and refreshing cocktails. Here are five white rum-based cocktails to try:

### MOJITO

A minty and refreshing mix of white rum, fresh lime juice, mint leaves, simple syrup, and soda water.

Ingredients:
- 2 oz white rum
- 1 oz fresh lime juice
- 8-10 mint leaves
- 1/2 oz simple syrup
- Soda water, to top
- Ice, for serving

Instructions:
1. Muddle 8-10 mint leaves and 1/2 oz of simple syrup in the bottom of a Collins glass.
2. Fill the glass with ice cubes.
3. Add 2 oz of white rum and 1 oz of fresh lime juice to the glass.
4. Stir the mixture gently.
5. Top with soda water.
6. Garnish the cocktail with a mint sprig.

## DAIQUIRI

A classic blend of white rum, lime juice, and simple syrup, shaken and strained into a chilled glass.

Ingredients:
- 2 oz white rum
- 1 oz lime juice
- 3/4 oz simple syrup
- Ice, for shaking

Instructions:
1. Fill a shaker with ice cubes.
2. Add 2 oz of white rum, 1 oz of lime juice, and 3/4 oz of simple syrup to the shaker.
3. Shake the mixture vigorously for 10-15 seconds.
4. Strain the mixture into a chilled cocktail glass.
5. Garnish the cocktail with a lime wheel or wedge.

## PIÑA COLADA

A tropical treat made with white rum, coconut cream, pineapple juice, and crushed ice, garnished with a pineapple wedge and cherry.

Ingredients:
- 2 oz white rum
- 1 1/2 oz coconut cream
- 3 oz pineapple juice
- Crushed ice, for blending
- Pineapple wedge and cherry, for garnish

Instructions:
1. Fill a blender with crushed ice.
2. Add 2 oz of white rum, 1 1/2 oz of coconut cream, and 3 oz of pineapple juice to the blender.
3. Blend the mixture until smooth.
4. Pour the mixture into a hurricane glass.
5. Garnish the cocktail with a pineapple wedge and cherry.

## CUBA LIBRE

A simple and satisfying mix of white rum, cola, and a squeeze of lime juice, garnished with a lime wedge.

Ingredients:

- 2 oz white rum
- Cola, to fill
- Squeeze of lime juice
- Lime wedge, for garnish
- Ice, for serving

Instructions:

1. Fill a highball glass with ice cubes.
2. Add 2 oz of white rum to the glass.
3. Squeeze a lime wedge into the glass.
4. Top with cola.
5. Stir the mixture gently.
6. Garnish the cocktail with a lime wedge.

### CAIPIRINHA

A Brazilian favorite made with white rum, muddled lime wedges, and sugar, served over crushed ice.

Ingredients:
- 2 oz white rum (traditionally made with cachaça)
- 1/2 lime, cut into wedges
- 2 tsp sugar
- Crushed ice, for serving

Instructions:
1. Cut half of a lime into wedges and place them in a rocks glass.
2. Add 2 tsp of sugar to the glass.
3. Muddle the lime wedges and sugar together until the sugar dissolves.
4. Fill the glass with crushed ice.
5. Add 2 oz of white rum to the glass.
6. Stir the mixture gently.
7. Garnish the cocktail with a lime wheel or wedge.

## WHITE WINE

White wine adds a crisp, fruity, and refreshing element to cocktails. It can be used as a base or a modifier to create a variety of delicious and sophisticated drinks. Here are five white wine-based cocktails to try:

### WHITE WINE SPRITZER

A light and effervescent blend of white wine and soda water, garnished with a lemon or orange wheel.

Ingredients:

- 4 oz white wine
- 2 oz soda water
- Lemon or orange wheel, for garnish

Instructions:

1. Fill a wine glass with ice cubes.
2. Add 4 oz of white wine to the glass.
3. Top with 2 oz of soda water.
4. Stir the mixture gently.
5. Garnish the cocktail with a lemon or orange wheel.

### SANGRIA BLANCA

A fruity and refreshing mix of white wine, brandy, orange liqueur, and assorted fresh fruit, topped with sparkling water or soda.

Ingredients:

- 1 bottle white wine
- 1/2 cup brandy
- 1/2 cup orange liqueur
- Assorted fresh fruit (e.g., apples, oranges, grapes, peaches)
- Sparkling water or soda, to top
- Ice, for serving

Instructions:

1. Slice assorted fresh fruit and place them in a pitcher.
2. Add 1/2 cup of brandy and 1/2 cup of orange liqueur to the pitcher.
3. Pour in 1 bottle of white wine and stir gently.
4. Let the mixture chill in the fridge for at least 30 minutes.
5. Fill glasses with ice cubes and pour the sangria mixture into the glasses.
6. Top with sparkling water or soda.
7. Garnish the cocktail with fresh fruit.

### WHITE WINE MARGARITA

A unique twist on the classic margarita, made with white wine, tequila, lime juice, and triple sec, garnished with a salted rim and lime wedge.

Ingredients:

- 3 oz white wine
- 1 oz tequila
- 1 oz lime juice
- 1 oz triple sec
- Salt, for rimming the glass
- Lime wedge, for garnish

Instructions:

1. Rim a chilled cocktail glass with salt.
2. Fill a shaker with ice cubes.
3. Add 3 oz of white wine, 1 oz of tequila, 1 oz of lime juice, and 1 oz of triple sec to the shaker.
4. Shake the mixture vigorously for 10-15 seconds.
5. Strain the mixture into the salt-rimmed glass.
6. Garnish the cocktail with a lime wedge.

### **APEROL SPRITZ**

A popular Italian aperitif, combining Prosecco, Aperol, and soda water, garnished with an orange slice.

Ingredients:
- 3 oz Prosecco
- 2 oz Aperol
- 1 oz soda water
- Orange slice, for garnish

Instructions:
1. Fill a wine glass with ice cubes.
2. Add 3 oz of Prosecco and 2 oz of Aperol to the glass.
3. Top with 1 oz of soda water.
4. Stir the mixture gently.
5. Garnish the cocktail with an orange slice.

## KIR ROYALE

Sophisticated and celebratory drink made with dry white wine or Champagne and a splash of crème de cassis, garnished with a lemon twist.

Ingredients:

- 4 oz dry white wine or Champagne
- 1/2 oz crème de cassis
- Lemon twist, for garnish

Instructions:

1. Chill a Champagne flute in the fridge or freezer.
2. Add 1/2 oz of crème de cassis to the bottom of the flute.
3. Slowly pour 4 oz of dry white wine or Champagne into the flute.
4. Stir the mixture gently.
5. Garnish the cocktail with a lemon twist.

By mastering these light spirit-based cocktails, you'll have a diverse range of recipes to impress your guests and cater to a variety of tastes. Whether you're hosting a summer party or a sophisticated soirée, these cocktails will provide the perfect accompaniment to any gathering.

## WHEN TO USE THESE PREFERRED SPIRITS

Light spirits such as vodka, gin, white rum, and white wine have long been popular choices for cocktails due to their versatility and ability to blend seamlessly with various flavors. Let's explore when these spirits are typically preferred or used in cocktail-making.

*Vodka:* Known for its clean, neutral taste, vodka is a go-to spirit for many cocktail enthusiasts. Its unassuming flavor profile allows it to mix well with a wide range of ingredients, making it an ideal choice for both simple and complex cocktails. Vodka-based cocktails are often enjoyed at social gatherings, parties, and during warm summer months due to their refreshing and easy-drinking nature. Examples of popular vodka cocktails include the Moscow Mule, Screwdriver, and Cosmopolitan.

*Gin:* Distilled from a variety of botanicals, gin offers a unique and complex flavor profile that lends itself well to a diverse array of cocktails. Its most notable characteristic is the distinct flavor of juniper berries, which often shines through in gin-based drinks. Gin cocktails are widely enjoyed at sophisticated events, garden parties, and, in the warmer months, as they tend to be refreshing and aromatic. Classic gin cocktails include the Gin & Tonic, Martini, and Tom Collins.

*White Rum:* Derived from sugarcane, white rum is a light, versatile spirit with a subtle sweetness that pairs well with a variety of mixers. White rum is commonly used in tropical and fruity cocktails, making it a popular choice for beachside vacations, pool parties, and summer gatherings. Iconic white rum cocktails include the Mojito, Piña Colada, and Daiquiri.

*White Wine:* White wine is typically crisp, refreshing, and can range in flavor from dry to sweet. It is often used as a base for wine cocktails or as a mixer in spritzes and punches. White wine-based cocktails are perfect for brunches, picnics, and warm-weather events due to their light, easy-drinking nature. Examples of white wine cocktails include the Wine Spritzer, Sangria Blanca, and Aperol Spritz.

In summary, light spirits like vodka, gin, white rum, and white wine are often preferred or used in cocktails that are refreshing, easy to drink and suitable for a range of occasions, particularly during warm-weather months and social gatherings.

## SPIRIT HISTORY

The Daiquiri, a classic cocktail made with white rum, lime juice, and simple syrup, has a fascinating origin story that dates back to the late 19th century. The cocktail is named after a beach near Santiago de Cuba, where it was said to be first concocted by an American mining engineer named Jennings Cox.

Cox found himself in Cuba during the Spanish-American War, working on a mining project in the area. One day, he invited some guests to his home for a party. Legend has it that he ran out of gin and decided to use the local Cuban rum as a substitute. To soften the strong taste of the rum, Cox added lime juice and sugar to create a refreshing and easy-to-drink concoction. The guests were impressed by this new cocktail, and the Daiquiri was born.

The Daiquiri gained popularity in the United States during the early 20th century, particularly during Prohibition, when Americans traveled to Cuba to enjoy the nightlife and sample cocktails that were forbidden back home. Famous figures like Ernest Hemingway and President John F. Kennedy were known to be fans of the Daiquiri, further contributing to its status as a classic cocktail.

This story exemplifies the versatility of light spirits like white rum and their ability to create refreshing, timeless cocktails. The Daiquiri's enduring popularity is a testament to the power of simple ingredients and the innovative spirit that lies at the heart of mixology.

## KEY TAKEAWAYS

We explored the world of light spirits, diving into the unique characteristics and uses of vodka, gin, white rum, and white wine in cocktail making. As you've learned, these spirits form the base of numerous classic cocktails and offer a wide range of possibilities for creative mixology. To summarize the most important points from this chapter, here are the key takeaways that will help you master the art of mixing light spirits in your cocktails:

- ***Versatility and flavor profiles:*** Light spirits like vodka, gin, white rum, and white wine are popular choices for cocktails due to their versatility and distinct flavor profiles. Each spirit brings unique characteristics to the drinks they are used in, making them suitable for a wide range of cocktails.
- ***Occasions and preferences:*** These light spirits are often preferred in cocktails that are served during warm-weather months, social gatherings, and various events such as sophisticated parties, brunches, and picnics. The light and refreshing nature of these spirits makes them suitable for easy-drinking cocktails that can be enjoyed on many occasions.
- ***Classic cocktails:*** Light spirits serve as the base for many classic cocktails, including the Moscow Mule (vodka), Gin & Tonic (gin), Mojito (white rum), and Wine Spritzer (white wine). These iconic drinks showcase the versatility and appeal of light spirits in the world of mixology.
- ***Innovation and creativity:*** The origin stories and histories of cocktails made with light spirits, such as the Daiquiri, demonstrate the innovative spirit of mixologists who have used these spirits to create timeless and beloved drinks.
- ***Experimentation and personalization:*** Understanding the characteristics and uses of light spirits empowers you to experiment with various flavor combinations, allowing you to create your own unique and enjoyable cocktails.

Now that you've become familiar with the key takeaways from Chapter 6, you have a solid foundation for mixing cocktails with light spirits. With a deeper understanding of their versatility, flavor profiles, and applications in various classic cocktails, you're well-equipped to experiment with different combinations and create your own refreshing concoctions. As you continue on your mixology journey, remember to embrace your creativity, as the world of light spirits offers endless possibilities for delightful and memorable drinks.

In the next chapter, we'll explore the world of dark spirits, including whiskey, bourbon, brandy, dark rum, and red wine. You'll learn how to create rich, complex, and satisfying cocktails that highlight the depth and warmth of these darker spirits, perfect for sipping by the fire or serving at a cozy dinner party. So, let's continue our mixology journey and delve into the enticing world of dark spirits!

# CHAPTER 7

## Mixing Dark Spirits

Indulge in the rich and complex flavors of dark spirits with these captivating recipes that celebrate the allure of whiskey, bourbon, brandy, dark rum, and red wine. Uncover the magic of mixology and create stunning cocktails with timeless appeal.

In this chapter, we will delve into the rich and complex world of dark spirits, including whiskey, bourbon, brandy, dark rum, and red wine. These spirits are characterized by their deeper flavors and often aged characteristics, making them ideal for creating cocktails that exude warmth, sophistication, and depth. Discover a variety of enticing cocktail recipes that showcase the unique qualities of each dark spirit, perfect for savoring on a chilly evening or sharing at an intimate gathering.

**WHISKEY**

Whiskey is a distilled spirit made from fermented grain mash, aged in oak barrels. Its rich, smoky, and complex flavors make it a popular choice for sipping neat or in a well-crafted cocktail. Here are five whiskey-based cocktails to try:

## OLD FASHIONED

A timeless and elegant mix of whiskey, sugar, Angostura bitters, and a splash of water, garnished with an orange peel and cherry.

Ingredients:

- 2 oz whiskey
- 1 sugar cube (or 0.5 oz simple syrup)
- 2 dashes Angostura bitters
- Splash of water
- Orange peel and cherry, for garnish

Instructions:

1. Place a sugar cube in an Old Fashioned glass (or use 0.5 oz of simple syrup).
2. Add 2 dashes of Angostura bitters to the glass.
3. Add a splash of water and muddle the sugar and bitters together until the sugar dissolves.
4. Fill the glass with ice cubes.
5. Add 2 oz of whiskey to the glass.
6. Stir the mixture gently.
7. Garnish the cocktail with an orange peel and cherry.

Whiskey Morgan

## WHISKEY SOUR

A classic blend of whiskey, lemon juice, simple syrup, and a dash of egg white, shaken and strained over ice, garnished with a lemon wheel and cherry.

Ingredients:

- 2 oz whiskey
- 0.75 oz fresh lemon juice
- 0.75 oz simple syrup
- Dash of egg white (optional)
- Lemon wheel and cherry, for garnish

Instructions:

1. Fill a shaker with ice cubes.
2. Add 2 oz of bourbon whiskey, 0.75 oz of fresh lemon juice, 0.75 oz of simple syrup, and a dash of egg white (optional) to the shaker.
3. Shake the mixture vigorously for 10-15 seconds.
4. Strain the mixture into a chilled rocks glass filled with ice.
5. Garnish the cocktail with a lemon wheel and cherry.

## MANHATTAN

A sophisticated concoction of whiskey, sweet vermouth, and Angostura bitters, stirred and strained into a chilled glass, garnished with a cherry.

Ingredients:

- 2 oz whiskey
- 1 oz sweet vermouth
- 2 dashes Angostura bitters
- Cherry, for garnish

Instructions:

1. Fill a mixing glass with ice cubes.
2. Add 2 oz of whiskey, 1 oz of sweet vermouth, and 2 dashes of Angostura bitters to the mixing glass.
3. Stir the mixture with a bar spoon for 20-30 seconds until well-chilled.
4. Strain the mixture into a chilled martini glass or rocks glass.
5. Garnish the cocktail with a cherry.

### MINT JULEP

A refreshing and minty mix of whiskey, fresh mint leaves, and simple syrup, served over crushed ice in a silver or pewter cup.

Ingredients:
- 2.5 oz whiskey
- 6-8 fresh mint leaves
- 0.5 oz simple syrup
- Crushed ice
- Mint sprig, for garnish

Instructions:
1. Muddle 6-8 fresh mint leaves and 0.5 oz of simple syrup in the bottom of a silver or pewter cup.
2. Fill the cup with crushed ice.
3. Add 2.5 oz of whiskey to the cup.
4. Stir the mixture gently until the outside of the cup frosts.
5. Top the cocktail with more crushed ice.
6. Garnish the cocktail with a mint sprig.

### ROB ROY

A smooth and smoky blend of Scotch whiskey, sweet vermouth, and Angostura bitters, stirred and strained into a chilled glass, garnished with a cherry.

Ingredients:
- 2 oz Scotch whiskey
- 1 oz sweet vermouth
- 2 dashes Angostura bitters
- Cherry, for garnish

Instructions:
1. Fill a mixing glass with ice cubes.
2. Add 2 oz of Scotch whiskey, 1 oz of sweet vermouth, and 2 dashes of Angostura bitters to the mixing glass.
3. Stir the mixture with a bar spoon for 20-30 seconds until well-chilled.
4. Strain the mixture into a chilled martini glass or rocks glass.
5. Garnish the cocktail with a cherry.

## BOURBON

Bourbon is a type of American whiskey made primarily from corn and aged in new, charred oak barrels. Its sweet and robust flavors make it a popular choice for classic and modern cocktails alike. Here are five bourbon-based cocktails to try:

### BOULEVARDIER

A rich and bittersweet mix of bourbon, Campari, and sweet vermouth, stirred and strained into a chilled glass, garnished with an orange peel.

Ingredients:
- 1.5 oz bourbon
- 1 oz Campari
- 1 oz sweet vermouth
- Orange peel, for garnish

Instructions:
1. Fill a mixing glass with ice cubes.
2. Add 1.5 oz of bourbon, 1 oz of Campari, and 1 oz of sweet vermouth to the mixing glass.
3. Stir the mixture with a bar spoon for 20-30 seconds until well-chilled.
4. Strain the mixture into a chilled rocks glass filled with ice.
5. Garnish the cocktail with an orange peel.

### KENTUCKY MULE

A refreshing blend of bourbon, ginger beer, and fresh lime juice, served over ice and garnished with a lime wedge.

Ingredients:

- 2 oz bourbon
- 4 oz ginger beer
- 0.5 oz fresh lime juice
- Lime wedge, for garnish

Instructions:

1. Fill a copper mug with ice cubes.
2. Add 2 oz of bourbon, 4 oz of ginger beer, and 0.5 oz of fresh lime juice to the mug.
3. Stir the mixture gently.
4. Garnish the cocktail with a lime wedge.

## WHISKEY SMASH

A fruity and minty mix of bourbon, lemon wedges, fresh mint leaves, and simple syrup, muddled and served over crushed ice.

Ingredients:

- 2 oz bourbon
- 3-4 lemon wedges
- 6-8 fresh mint leaves
- 0.5 oz simple syrup
- Crushed ice, for serving

Instructions:

1. Muddle 3-4 lemon wedges, 6-8 fresh mint leaves, and 0.5 oz of simple syrup in the bottom of a rocks glass.
2. Fill the glass with crushed ice.
3. Add 2 oz of bourbon to the glass.
4. Stir the mixture gently.
5. Garnish the cocktail with a lemon wedge and mint leaves.

## BROWN DERBY

A smooth and tangy blend of bourbon, grapefruit juice, and honey syrup, shaken and strained into a chilled glass.

Ingredients:
- 2 oz bourbon
- 1 oz fresh grapefruit juice
- 0.5 oz honey syrup (equal parts honey and water, heated until combined)
- Grapefruit twist, for garnish

Instructions:
1. Fill a shaker with ice cubes.
2. Add 2 oz of bourbon, 1 oz of fresh grapefruit juice, and 0.5 oz of honey syrup to the shaker.
3. Shake the mixture vigorously for 10-15 seconds.
4. Strain the mixture into a chilled rocks glass.
5. Garnish the cocktail with a grapefruit twist.

## PAPER PLANE

A well-balanced and bright mix of bourbon, Aperol, Amaro Nonino, and fresh lemon juice, shaken and strained into a chilled glass.

Ingredients:
- 0.75 oz bourbon
- 0.75 oz Aperol
- 0.75 oz Amaro Nonino
- 0.75 oz fresh lemon juice

Instructions:
1. Fill a shaker with ice cubes.
2. Add 0.75 oz of bourbon, 0.75 oz of Aperol, 0.75 oz of Amaro Nonino, and 0.75 oz of fresh lemon juice to the shaker.
3. Shake the mixture vigorously for 10-15 seconds.
4. Strain the mixture into a chilled martini glass or rocks glass.
5. Garnish the cocktail with a lemon twist.

## BRANDY

Brandy is a distilled spirit made from fermented fruit juice, typically grapes, and aged in oak barrels. Its rich, fruity, and warming flavors make it an ideal base for a variety of cocktails. Here are five brandy-based cocktails to try:

### SIDECAR

A classic and elegant mix of brandy, orange liqueur, and lemon juice, shaken and strained into a sugar-rimmed glass.

Ingredients:

- 2 oz brandy (such as Cognac or Armagnac)
- 1 oz orange liqueur (such as Cointreau or Grand Marnier)
- 0.75 oz fresh lemon juice
- Sugar, for rimming the glass

Instructions:

1. Rim a chilled cocktail glass with sugar.
2. Fill a shaker with ice cubes.
3. Add 2 oz of brandy, 1 oz of orange liqueur, and 0.75 oz of fresh lemon juice to the shaker.
4. Shake the mixture vigorously for 10-15 seconds.
5. Strain the mixture into the sugar-rimmed cocktail glass.
6. Garnish the cocktail with a lemon twist.

Whiskey Morgan

## BRANDY ALEXANDER

A creamy and indulgent blend of brandy, crème de cacao, and heavy cream, shaken and strained into a chilled glass, garnished with a dusting of nutmeg.

Ingredients:

- 1.5 oz brandy (such as Cognac or Armagnac)
- 1 oz crème de cacao (dark)
- 1 oz heavy cream
- Nutmeg, for garnish

Instructions:

1. Fill a shaker with ice cubes.
2. Add 1.5 oz of brandy, 1 oz of crème de cacao, and 1 oz of heavy cream to the shaker.
3. Shake the mixture vigorously for 10-15 seconds.
4. Strain the mixture into a chilled cocktail glass.
5. Garnish the cocktail with a dusting of nutmeg.

## STINGER

A simple and refreshing mix of brandy and crème de menthe, shaken and strained over ice.

Ingredients:

- 2 oz brandy (such as Cognac or Armagnac)
- 0.5 oz crème de menthe (white)
- Crushed ice, for serving

Instructions:

1. Fill a shaker with ice cubes.
2. Add 2 oz of brandy and 0.5 oz of crème de menthe to the shaker.
3. Shake the mixture vigorously for 10-15 seconds.
4. Strain the mixture into a chilled rocks glass filled with crushed ice.
5. Garnish the cocktail with a sprig of fresh mint (optional).

## FRENCH CONNECTION

A smooth and sophisticated blend of brandy and amaretto, served neat in an old-fashioned glass.

Ingredients:

- 1.5 oz brandy (such as Cognac or Armagnac)
- 1.5 oz amaretto

Instructions:

1. Fill an old-fashioned glass with ice cubes.
2. Add 1.5 oz of brandy and 1.5 oz of amaretto to the glass.
3. Stir the mixture gently.
4. Garnish the cocktail with a lemon twist or orange peel (optional).

### BRANDY DAISY

A bright and zesty mix of brandy, lemon juice, simple syrup, and grenadine, shaken and strained into a chilled glass, garnished with a lemon twist and cherry.

Ingredients:
- 2 oz brandy (such as Cognac or Armagnac)
- 0.75 oz fresh lemon juice
- 0.5 oz simple syrup
- 0.25 oz grenadine
- Lemon twist and maraschino cherry, for garnish

Instructions:
1. Fill a shaker with ice cubes.
2. Add 2 oz of brandy, 0.75 oz of fresh lemon juice, 0.5 oz of simple syrup, and 0.25 oz of grenadine to the shaker.
3. Shake the mixture vigorously for 10-15 seconds.
4. Strain the mixture into a chilled cocktail glass.
5. Garnish the cocktail with a lemon twist and maraschino cherry.

## DARK RUM

Dark rum is a distilled spirit made from sugarcane byproducts, such as molasses, and aged in oak barrels. Its rich, bold, and slightly sweet flavors make it a versatile choice for a range of cocktails. Here are five dark rum-based cocktails to try:

### DARK 'N' STORMY

A refreshing and spicy blend of dark rum, ginger beer, and a squeeze of lime, served over ice and garnished with a lime wedge.

Ingredients:

- 2 oz dark rum (such as Gosling's Black Seal)
- 4 oz ginger beer
- 0.5 oz fresh lime juice
- Lime wedge, for garnish

Instructions:

1. Fill a highball glass with ice.
2. Pour 2 oz of dark rum into the glass.
3. Add 0.5 oz of fresh lime juice.
4. Top the glass with 4 oz of ginger beer and stir gently.
5. Garnish with a lime wedge.

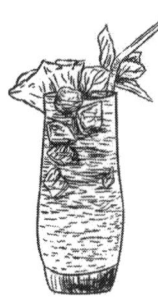

## MAI TAI

A tropical and fruity mix of dark rum, light rum, orange curaçao, orgeat syrup, and lime juice, shaken and strained over crushed ice, garnished with a sprig of mint and a cherry.

Ingredients:

- 1 oz dark rum (such as Myers's)
- 1 oz light rum (such as Bacardi Silver)
- 0.5 oz orange curaçao
- 0.5 oz orgeat syrup
- 1 oz fresh lime juice
- Mint sprig and cherry, for garnish

Instructions:

1. Fill a cocktail shaker with ice.
2. Add 1 oz of dark rum, 1 oz of light rum, 0.5 oz of orange curaçao, 0.5 oz of orgeat syrup, and 1 oz of fresh lime juice to the shaker.
3. Shake vigorously for 10-15 seconds.
4. Fill a rocks glass with crushed ice.
5. Strain the cocktail over the ice.
6. Garnish with a sprig of mint and a cherry.

Whiskey Morgan

## RUM OLD FASHIONED

A rich and aromatic twist on the classic Old Fashioned, made with dark rum, sugar, Angostura bitters, and a splash of water, garnished with an orange peel and cherry.

Ingredients:

- 2 oz dark rum (such as Mount Gay or El Dorado)
- 1 sugar cube or 0.5 oz simple syrup
- 2 dashes Angostura bitters
- Splash of water
- Orange peel and maraschino cherry, for garnish

Instructions:

1. In an old-fashioned glass, add 1 sugar cube or 0.5 oz of simple syrup and 2 dashes of Angostura bitters.
2. Add a splash of water and stir until the sugar is dissolved.
3. Fill the glass with ice.
4. Pour 2 oz of dark rum into the glass and stir gently.
5. Garnish with an orange peel and a maraschino cherry.

## ZOMBIE

A potent and complex blend of dark rum, light rum, apricot brandy, lime juice, pineapple juice, and grenadine, shaken and strained into a tall glass filled with crushed ice.

Ingredients:
- 1 oz dark rum (such as Appleton Estate)
- 1 oz light rum (such as Bacardi Silver)
- 0.5 oz apricot brandy
- 1 oz fresh lime juice
- 1 oz pineapple juice
- 0.5 oz grenadine
- Pineapple wedge or cherry, for garnish (optional)

Instructions:
1. Fill a cocktail shaker with ice.
2. Add 1 oz of dark rum, 1 oz of light rum, 0.5 oz of apricot brandy, 1 oz of fresh lime juice, 1 oz of pineapple juice, and 0.5 oz of grenadine to the shaker.
3. Shake vigorously for 10-15 seconds.
4. Fill a tall glass with crushed ice.
5. Strain the cocktail over the ice.
6. Garnish with a pineapple wedge or cherry (optional).

### EL PRESIDENTE

A smooth and sophisticated mix of dark rum, orange curaçao, dry vermouth, and a dash of grenadine, stirred and strained into a chilled glass.

Ingredients:
- 2 oz dark rum (such as Havana Club 7-year)
- 0.75 oz orange curaçao
- 0.75 oz dry vermouth (such as Noilly Prat)
- 1 dash grenadine
- Orange twist, for garnish (optional)

Instructions:
1. Fill a mixing glass with ice.
2. Add 2 oz of dark rum, 0.75 oz of orange curaçao, 0.75 oz of dry vermouth, and a dash of grenadine to the glass.
3. Stir the mixture for 10-15 seconds.
4. Strain the cocktail into a chilled glass.
5. Garnish with an orange twist (optional).

## RED WINE

Red wine is a popular choice for adding depth and complexity to cocktails. Its rich, fruity, and tannic flavors make it an excellent complement to a variety of ingredients. Here are five red wine-based cocktails to try:

### NEW YORK SOUR

A bold and tangy blend of whiskey, lemon juice, simple syrup, and a red wine float, shaken and strained into a chilled glass.

Ingredients:
- 2 oz whiskey (such as bourbon or rye)
- 1 oz fresh lemon juice
- 0.5 oz simple syrup
- 0.5 oz red wine (such as Malbec or Shiraz)
- Lemon or orange twist, for garnish

Instructions:
1. Fill a cocktail shaker with ice.
2. Add 2 oz whiskey, 1 oz fresh lemon juice, and 0.5 oz simple syrup.
3. Shake well.
4. Strain the mixture into a chilled glass filled with ice.
5. Gently pour 0.5 oz red wine over the back of a spoon to float on top of the cocktail.
6. Garnish with a lemon or orange twist.

Whiskey Morgan

## MULLED WINE

A warming and spiced concoction of red wine, brandy, orange slices, and a mix of spices such as cinnamon, cloves, and star anise, gently heated and served warm.

Ingredients:

- 1 bottle red wine (such as Cabernet Sauvignon or Merlot)
- 0.5 cup brandy
- 1 orange, sliced
- 2 cinnamon sticks
- 8 whole cloves
- 3 whole star anise
- 0.25 cup sugar or honey, to taste (optional)

Instructions:

1. Combine 1 bottle of red wine, 0.5 cup brandy, 1 sliced orange, 2 cinnamon sticks, 8 whole cloves, and 3 whole star anise in a large pot.
2. Heat the mixture over low heat until it begins to steam, but not boil.
3. Let the mixture simmer for at least 30 minutes to allow the flavors to meld together.
4. Strain the mulled wine into heatproof glasses or mugs.
5. Add sugar or honey to taste, if desired.

## SANGRIA

A fruity and refreshing mix of red wine, brandy, orange juice, and an assortment of fresh fruit, served over ice.

Ingredients:

- 1 bottle red wine (such as Rioja or Tempranillo)
- 0.5 cup brandy
- 1 cup orange juice
- Assorted fresh fruit (such as oranges, lemons, apples, and berries)
- 0.25 cup sugar or simple syrup, to taste (optional)
- Club soda, to top (optional)

Instructions:

1. In a large pitcher, combine 1 bottle of red wine, 0.5 cup brandy, 1 cup orange juice, and assorted fresh fruit.
2. Stir well.
3. Refrigerate the mixture for at least 2 hours or overnight to allow the flavors to meld together.
4. When ready to serve, add ice to glasses and pour the sangria over the ice.
5. Top with club soda, if desired.
6. Add sugar or simple syrup to taste, if desired.
7. Garnish with additional fresh fruit.

**RED WINE SPRITZER**

A light and fizzy blend of red wine and soda water, served over ice and garnished with a lemon twist.

Ingredients:
- 4 oz red wine (such as Pinot Noir or Merlot)
- 2 oz soda water
- Lemon twist, for garnish

Instructions:
1. Fill a glass with ice.
2. Add 4 oz red wine and 2 oz soda water.
3. Stir gently.
4. Garnish with a lemon twist.

## BISHOP

A zesty and aromatic mix of red wine, dark rum, lime juice, and simple syrup, served over ice and garnished with a lime wheel and a cherry.

Ingredients:
- 4 oz red wine (such as Cabernet Sauvignon or Zinfandel)
- 1 oz dark rum
- 1 oz fresh lime juice
- 0.5 oz simple syrup
- Lime wheel and cherry, for garnish

Instructions:
1. Fill a glass with ice.
2. Add 4 oz red wine, 1 oz dark rum, 1 oz fresh lime juice, and 0.5 oz simple syrup.
3. Stir well.
4. Garnish with a lime wheel and cherry.

With these dark spirit-based cocktails under your belt, you'll be well-equipped to create a variety of satisfying and sophisticated drinks for any occasion. Whether you're curling up by the fire or hosting a cozy dinner party, these cocktails are sure to impress and delight your guests.

## WHEN TO USE THESE PREFERRED SPIRITS

Dark spirits, such as whiskey, bourbon, brandy, dark rum, and red wine, are often preferred in cocktails that are consumed during cooler weather or in more intimate settings. These spirits bring warmth, complexity, and depth of flavor to the cocktails they are used in, making them perfect for sipping slowly by a fireplace or during a dinner party. Their rich and robust characteristics lend themselves well to drinks that are meant to be savored, and they are often used in cocktails with a slightly more complex flavor profile.

## SPIRIT HISTORY

The Sazerac, a classic cocktail originating in New Orleans, is a prime example of how dark spirits can be used to create a drink with a rich history and a unique flavor profile. The Sazerac was first made in the early 19th century and originally called for cognac, a type of brandy, as its primary ingredient. However, when the phylloxera epidemic devastated French vineyards in the 1870s, bartenders in New Orleans began using rye whiskey as a substitute, and the modern Sazerac was born.

The Sazerac is a potent combination of rye whiskey (or cognac), sugar, Peychaud's bitters, a dash of absinthe, and a lemon twist. The drink is served in an old-fashioned glass, and its rich, spicy flavors have made it an enduring symbol of New Orleans' cocktail culture. The story of the Sazerac illustrates how dark spirits can adapt to changing circumstances and contribute to the evolution of classic cocktails.

## KEY TAKEAWAYS

We delved into the fascinating world of dark spirits, exploring the unique qualities and applications of whiskey, bourbon, brandy, dark rum, and red wine in the realm of mixology. These spirits, with their rich and complex flavors, form the foundation of many classic cocktails and provide a wealth of opportunities for creative drink-making. To help you better understand and appreciate the versatility and depth of dark spirits, here are the key takeaways from this chapter:

- *Ideal occasions:* Dark spirits like whiskey, bourbon, brandy, dark rum, and red wine are often preferred in cocktails that are consumed during cooler weather, intimate gatherings, and dinner parties. Their warm and complex flavors make them suitable for slow sipping and contemplative enjoyment.
- *Rich and complex flavors:* The depth and robustness of dark spirits make them ideal for creating cocktails with a more intricate flavor profile, adding warmth and complexity to the drinks they are used in.
- *Classic cocktails:* Dark spirits serve as the base for many iconic cocktails, such as the Old Fashioned (whiskey), Manhattan (bourbon), Sidecar (brandy), Dark 'n' Stormy (dark rum), and Sangria (red wine). These classic drinks showcase the versatility and appeal of dark spirits in mixology.
- *Adaptability and evolution:* The history of cocktails like the Sazerac demonstrates how dark spirits have been adapted and substituted in response to changing circumstances, contributing to the continuous evolution of the cocktail world.
- *Experimentation and personalization:* Understanding the characteristics and uses of dark spirits empowers you to experiment with various flavor combinations and create your own unique, satisfying cocktails that showcase the warmth and depth these spirits have to offer.

Armed with the key takeaways from Chapter 7, you now have a solid understanding of dark spirits and their role in crafting delectable cocktails. By appreciating the depth, complexity, and history of these spirits, you can create cocktails that showcase their unique characteristics and offer a memorable drinking experience. As you continue on your mixology journey, don't be afraid to experiment and personalize your concoctions with dark spirits, as they provide endless possibilities for creating cocktails that are both comforting and captivating.

In the next chapter, we'll explore the art of infusing classic cocktails with unique and unexpected flavors, providing you with ten innovative recipes to elevate your mixology skills and wow your friends and family. Let's continue our mixology adventure and get ready to infuse your classic cocktails with a creative twist!

# CHAPTER 8
## Infusing Classic Cocktails

Classic cocktails meet modern innovation in this tantalizing chapter, where we'll reveal 10 unique recipes that infuse traditional favorites with exciting twists. Unleash your creativity and embark on a mixology adventure that knows no bounds!

In this chapter, we'll explore the art of infusing classic cocktails with unique and unexpected flavors. By experimenting with various ingredients and techniques, you can elevate your mixology skills and create innovative drinks that will wow your friends and family.

By taking well-loved drinks and adding unexpected elements, mixologists can create innovative concoctions that pay homage to their classic roots while offering a refreshing change of pace. To understand the process and creativity behind these infused creations, we'll explore the art of cocktail infusion and share some fascinating stories and facts that exemplify this innovative approach to mixology.

Here are ten infused cocktail recipes that put a creative twist on classic cocktails:

### LAVENDER COLLINS

Add a floral touch to the classic Tom Collins by infusing your gin with lavender. To make the infusion, simply combine gin and dried lavender buds in a jar, seal, and let it sit for 24-48 hours. Strain out the lavender and use the infused gin in your Tom Collins recipe.

Ingredients:
- 2 oz lavender-infused gin
- 1 oz fresh lemon juice
- 0.5 oz simple syrup
- Club soda, to top
- Lemon wheel and lavender sprig, for garnish

Instructions:
1. Combine 2 cups of gin and 1/4 cup of dried lavender buds in a jar, seal, and let it sit for 24-48 hours.
2. Strain out the lavender and measure 2 oz of the infused gin into a shaker.
3. Add 1 oz of fresh lemon juice, 0.5 oz of simple syrup, and ice (about 1 cup) to the shaker and shake well.
4. Strain into a Collins glass filled with ice.
5. Top with club soda and garnish with a lemon wheel and lavender sprig.

## JALAPEÑO MARGARITA

Add a spicy kick to the classic Margarita by muddling a few slices of fresh jalapeño in the shaker before adding the tequila, orange liqueur, and lime juice. Shake and strain into a salt-rimmed glass for a fiery and refreshing twist on the original.

Ingredients:

- 2 oz tequila
- 1 oz orange liqueur (such as Cointreau or Triple Sec)
- 1 oz fresh lime juice
- 1-2 slices fresh jalapeño, muddled
- Salt, for rimming the glass
- Lime wedge, for garnish

Instructions:

1. Rim a glass with salt and fill it with ice.
2. Muddle 1-2 slices of fresh jalapeño in a shaker.
3. Add 2 oz of tequila, 1 oz of orange liqueur (such as Cointreau or Triple Sec), 1 oz of fresh lime juice, and ice (about 1 cup) to the shaker and shake well.
4. Strain into the prepared glass.
5. Garnish with a lime wedge.

### SMOKED OLD FASHIONED

Impart a smoky flavor to your Old Fashioned by first smoking your glass. To do this, light a small piece of wood or a smoking gun, place the lit end under an overturned glass, and let it fill with smoke. Quickly turn the glass upright, mix your Old Fashioned, and pour it into the smoked glass.

Ingredients:

- 2 oz bourbon or rye whiskey
- 0.5 oz simple syrup
- 2 dashes Angostura bitters
- Orange or lemon peel, for garnish
- Maraschino cherry, for garnish

Instructions:

1. Light a small piece of wood or a smoking gun and place it under an overturned glass to smoke it.
2. In a separate glass, mix 2 oz of bourbon or rye whiskey, 0.5 oz of simple syrup, and 2 dashes of Angostura bitters.
3. Turn the smoked glass upright and strain the mixed cocktail into it.
4. Garnish with a twist of orange or lemon peel and a maraschino cherry.

### EARL GREY MARTINI

Infuse your gin with the delicate flavor of Earl Grey tea for a sophisticated take on the classic Martini. Simply steep an Earl Grey tea bag in gin for 2-3 hours, then remove the tea bag and use the infused gin in your Martini recipe.

Ingredients:
- 2 oz Earl Grey-infused gin
- 0.5 oz dry vermouth
- Lemon twist, for garnish

Instructions:
1. Steep an Earl Grey tea bag in 2 cups of gin for 2-3 hours.
2. Remove the tea bag and measure 2 oz of the infused gin into a shaker.
3. Add 0.5 oz of dry vermouth, ice (about 1 cup), and shake well.
4. Strain into a chilled martini glass.
5. Garnish with a lemon twist.

## BASIL MOJITO

Upgrade your Mojito by muddling fresh basil leaves along with the mint for a fresh and fragrant twist on the classic. The basil adds an herbaceous depth that complements the rum, lime, and mint flavors.

Ingredients:
- 2 oz white rum
- 1 oz fresh lime juice
- 0.5 oz simple syrup
- 6-8 fresh mint leaves
- 4-5 fresh basil leaves
- Club soda, to top
- Mint sprig and lime wheel, for garnish

Instructions:
1. Muddle 6-8 fresh mint leaves and 4-5 fresh basil leaves in a shaker.
2. Add 2 oz of white rum, 1 oz of fresh lime juice, 0.5 oz of simple syrup, and ice (about 1 cup) to the shaker and shake well.
3. Strain into a glass filled with ice.
4. Top with club soda and garnish with a mint sprig and lime wheel.

## EASTSIDE

Add a cool and refreshing twist to the classic Gimlet by muddling cucumber and mint leaves in the shaker before adding the gin and lime juice. Shake and strain into a chilled glass for a crisp and invigorating variation.

Ingredients:

- 2 oz gin
- 1 oz fresh lime juice
- 0.5 oz simple syrup
- 3-4 cucumber slices
- 4-5 fresh mint leaves
- Cucumber slice and mint sprig, for garnish

Instructions:

1. Muddle 3-4 cucumber slices and 4-5 fresh mint leaves in a shaker.
2. Add 2 oz of gin, 1 oz of fresh lime juice, 0.5 oz of simple syrup, and ice (about 1 cup) to the shaker and shake well.
3. Strain into a chilled glass.
4. Garnish with a cucumber slice and a mint sprig.

### BLACKBERRY BOURBON SMASH

Enhance your Whiskey Smash by muddling fresh blackberries along with the lemon wedges and mint leaves. The blackberries add a burst of fruity flavor that pairs beautifully with the bourbon and mint.

Ingredients:
- 2 oz bourbon
- 0.5 oz simple syrup
- 3-4 lemon wedges
- 3-4 fresh blackberries
- 4-5 fresh mint leaves
- Mint sprig and blackberry, for garnish

Instructions:
1. Muddle 3-4 fresh blackberries, 3-4 lemon wedges, and 4-5 fresh mint leaves in a shaker.
2. Add 2 oz of bourbon, 0.5 oz of simple syrup, and ice (about 1 cup) to the shaker and shake well.
3. Strain into a glass filled with ice.
4. Garnish with a mint sprig and a fresh blackberry.

### ROSEMARY AND GRAPEFRUIT PALOMA

Elevate your Paloma by infusing your tequila with rosemary. Combine tequila and fresh rosemary sprigs in a jar, seal, and let it sit for 24-48 hours. Strain out the rosemary and use the infused tequila in your Paloma recipe, which includes grapefruit juice, lime juice, and a splash of soda water.

Ingredients:
- 2 oz rosemary-infused tequila
- 2 oz fresh grapefruit juice
- 0.5 oz fresh lime juice
- Club soda, to top
- Salt, for rimming the glass
- Grapefruit wedge and rosemary sprig, for garnish

Instructions:
1. Combine 2 cups of tequila and 4-5 fresh rosemary sprigs in a jar, seal, and let it sit for 24-48 hours.
2. Strain out the rosemary and measure 2 oz of the infused tequila into a shaker.
3. Add 2 oz of fresh grapefruit juice, 0.5 oz of fresh lime juice, 0.5 oz of simple syrup, and ice (about 1 cup) to the shaker and shake well.
4. Strain into a glass filled with ice.
5. Top with club soda and garnish with a grapefruit wedge and a rosemary sprig.

## CARDAMOM AND ORANGE NEGRONI

Add a spicy and fragrant twist to your Negroni by infusing your gin with crushed cardamom pods. Combine gin and cardamom in a jar, seal, and let it sit for 24 hours. Strain out the cardamom and use the infused gin in your Negroni recipe, which includes equal parts gin, Campari, and sweet vermouth.

Ingredients:

- 1 oz cardamom-infused gin
- 1 oz Campari
- 1 oz sweet vermouth
- Orange twist, for garnish

Instructions:

1. Combine 2 cups of gin and 1/4 cup of crushed cardamom pods in a jar, seal, and let it sit for 24 hours.
2. Strain out the cardamom and measure 1 oz of the infused gin into a shaker.
3. Add 1 oz of Campari, 1 oz of sweet vermouth, and ice (about 1 cup) to the shaker and stir well.
4. Strain into a glass filled with ice.
5. Garnish with an orange twist.

Whiskey Morgan

### VANILLA ESPRESSO MARTINI

Give your Espresso Martini a velvety touch by infusing your vodka with vanilla beans. Split a vanilla bean lengthwise, scrape out the seeds, and add both the seeds and the pod to a jar of vodka. Seal and let it sit for 5-7 days before straining and using the infused vodka in your Espresso Martini recipe.

Ingredients:
- 2 oz vanilla-infused vodka
- 1 oz freshly brewed espresso, cooled
- 0.5 oz coffee liqueur (such as Kahlúa)
- 0.5 oz simple syrup
- 3 whole coffee beans, for garnish

Instructions:
1. Split 1 vanilla bean lengthwise, scrape out the seeds, and add both the seeds and the pod to 2 cups of vodka. Seal and let it sit for 5-7 days before straining.
2. Add 2 oz of vanilla-infused vodka, 1 oz of freshly brewed espresso (cooled), 0.5 oz of coffee liqueur (such as Kahlúa), 0.5 oz of simple syrup, and ice (about 1 cup) to a shaker and shake well.
3. Strain into a chilled glass.
4. Garnish with 3 whole coffee beans.

**KEY TAKEAWAYS**

In this chapter, we explored the fascinating world of infused classic cocktails, where familiar drinks are given new life through imaginative twists and innovative techniques. By understanding the principles of infusion and learning about the unique stories behind these creations, you can appreciate the ingenuity and skill that goes into crafting these delicious concoctions. Here are the key takeaways from this chapter:

- The art of infusing classic cocktails involves taking familiar drinks and adding creative twists, unexpected flavors, or innovative techniques to create a unique and memorable experience.
- Infusing classic cocktails requires a deep understanding of the original drink's flavor profile and balance to ensure that the added elements enhance, rather than detract from, the overall taste.

- Experimenting with different ingredients, such as herbs, spices, fruits, and even smoke, can lead to the discovery of intriguing flavor combinations and inspire new cocktail creations.
- The infusion process can involve a variety of techniques, such as muddling, steeping, fat-washing, or using specialized equipment like a smoking gun, to achieve the desired result.
- Infused classic cocktails pay homage to their traditional roots while offering a refreshing and innovative take on well-loved drinks, showcasing the endless possibilities in the world of mixology.

With the key takeaways from Chapter 8 in mind, you are now equipped to appreciate and explore the world of infused classic cocktails. By understanding the principles and techniques behind these innovative drinks, you can experiment with infusing your own concoctions and discover the endless possibilities that lie within the world of mixology. As you continue to develop your skills and knowledge, remember that the key to successful infusion lies in creativity, balance, and a deep understanding of both classic and novel flavors.

By experimenting with infusions and creative flavor combinations, you can breathe new life into classic cocktails and impress your guests with your mixology skills. As you gain experience and confidence, don't be afraid to try your own unique infusions and flavor pairings. The key is to balance the flavors, respect the essence of the classic cocktail, and let your creativity shine.

# CONCLUSION

Throughout this book, we've delved into the fascinating world of mixology, focusing on classic cocktails and the knowledge and skills required to create them at home. From studying the history of classic cocktails to curating your arsenal of ingredients and learning essential techniques, you've embarked on a journey to become a skilled at-home bartender.

Now that you've equipped yourself with the necessary tools, glassware, and ingredients, you're ready to start crafting delicious and impressive cocktails for yourself and your loved ones. As you continue to hone your skills, remember to experiment with new flavors, techniques, and presentation styles. The world of mixology is vast and ever evolving, and the more you learn and explore, the more you'll grow as a home bartender.

Ever dreamt of crafting signature cocktails that leave a lasting impression? Now you can! You've learned how to personalize classic recipes and design your own show-stopping drinks that are sure to wow your guests and leave them craving more. The possibilities are endless!

So, raise a glass to your newfound mixology knowledge, and get ready to shake, stir, and sip your way to bartending success. Cheers!

## A SHORT MESSAGE FROM THE AUTHOR

Hey, are you enjoying the book? I'd love to hear your thoughts!

Many readers do not know how hard reviews are to come by, and how much they help an author.

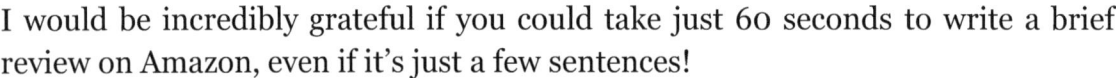

I would be incredibly grateful if you could take just 60 seconds to write a brief review on Amazon, even if it's just a few sentences!

\>> Click here to leave a quick review

Thank you for taking the time to share your thoughts!

Your review will genuinely make a difference for me and help gain exposure for my work.

Whiskey Morgan